P9-ARV-883

Praise for *"I'll Give You Exactly Five Minutes!"*

"The ORSON System is a brilliant approach to public speaking from the most outstanding presentation coach I have ever worked with. Peter Danish provides no-nonsense and actionable advice, for anyone and everyone, on how to effectively deliver a speech in order to win over an audience. The ORSON System is simple to use, yet it delivers powerful results!"

- Joe Peyronnin
former President Fox News, Vice President CBS News

"Taking the stage after working with Peter is not just effective, but fun! With gentle humor, firm resolve, and genuine skill, he coaches you to a level of confidence that lets you know, even as you are connecting with your audience, that your message is getting across, and that the sale -- be it of an idea, product, or service -- is about to happen."

- Carmen M. DiRienzo
Founding CEO of V-me Media

"Peter is an absolutely brilliant marketing strategist who has a unique and keen understanding of every phase of our industry. This is a rare commodity in these days of "specialists" that possess great knowledge in one area of the business without the perspective of how everything works in the grand scheme of things. Moreover, Peter is creative, eloquent, exceptionally intelligent and has great interpersonal skills. You'd be hard pressed to find someone with a better reputation throughout our business."

- Tom Marsillo
CEO of Emerging Networks

"Peter cuts to the chase and executes improvement more efficiently than anyone with whom I've worked. If you're interested in improving your presentation and communication skills quickly and in a sustainable fashion, talk to him right away."

- Richard Taub
Chief Financial Officer, V-me TV Networks

"A good presentation is a theater piece that will take an audience on a rewarding journey. Peter Danish's simple rules are an excellent framework on which to craft your message."

- Brian Maffitt
CEO, Total Training Inc. and frequent keynote speaker

"As a professional musician, I've spent almost half my life on stage and I really thought I knew all there was to know about engaging an audience. Now, as a business owner, I've found it's a whole different ballgame. Peter has helped bring my presentation skills to a new level with his easy to use practical ORSON system."

- Joe D'Urso
Owner of CBGB's & Caravan Management

"Have a speech coming up? Giving a major presentation? Need to get your sales team pumped? Call Peter. He's a pro at crafting the best copy, appropriate messaging, or a motivating rally cry. And he'll assist every step of the way. From initial ideation to presentation development to delivery coaching. You'll be glad he's part of your team."

- Carla Trum Mercado
President of MGSCOMM Advertising

"Whether you're a scarecrow looking for courage, a lion longing for heart, a tin man praying for a brain, or a Dorothy hoping to bring a message home, when it comes to presentation skills, Peter Danish is the wizard with all the answers. His talents are nothing less than magic."

- Court Stroud
Senior Vice President of Azteca TV

"Peter Danish is a jack of all trades and a master of most. He is one of the most creative individuals I have ever encountered. Whenever I have a large scale presentation to give, he is always the first person I call."

- Stephen J. Levin
EVP Sales Telemundo Network

"Peter takes the theories taught in a business communication course and boils them down to practical principles that will have you making more effective and efficient presentations after just one reading."

- Dr. Jay Sholes, PhD.
Pace University

"**I'll Give You Exactly 5 Minutes** is the only book on giving presentations that I have read which gives you a real and candid approach to presenting for modern day situations, without the fluff. This book teaches you to how to present, leveraging your personality type and building off of that to make the perfect presentation. I can truly relate to the unsung presenting tips addressed in this book. Spectacular!"

- Lance Rios
President and CEO of Being Latino.com, Hispanicize.com

"Most people are in the business of selling one product or another. Peter is in the business of selling ideas – and he can help you sell ideas. In this book, he mixes his creative background with his extensive business experience to offer a practical approach to business communication. Use O.R.S.O.N. to clarify your thoughts, simplify your life and get your ideas across!"

- Robert Brown

President, CEO Credos Communications Associates

"Peter is the Real Deal. When it comes to large scale presentations he is second to none. He moves effortlessly between speech writer/ coach/producer/creative. His expertise goes far beyond just delivery and presentation; he provides invaluable help with content, clarity and organization. He delivers!"

- Manuel Abud

CEO of Azteca Television Network

"I'LL GIVE YOU EXACTLY FIVE MINUTES!"

A Guide to the ORSON System of Presentation

PETER DANISH

Nyack Library
59 South Broadway
Nyack, NY 10960-3834

MOtivational PRESS
LEADERS IN GLOBAL PUBLISHING

Published by Motivational Press, Inc.
1777 Aurora Road
Melbourne, Florida, 32935
www.MotivationalPress.com

Copyright 2015 © Peter Danish
All Rights Reserved

No part of this book may be reproduced or transmitted in any form by any means: graphic, electronic, or mechanical, including photocopying, recording, taping or by any information storage or retrieval system without permission, in writing, from the authors, except for the inclusion of brief quotations in a review, article, book, or academic paper. The authors and publisher of this book and the associated materials have used their best efforts in preparing this material. The authors and publisher make no representations or warranties with respect to accuracy, applicability, fitness or completeness of the contents of this material. They disclaim any warranties expressed or implied, merchantability, or fitness for any particular purpose. The authors and publisher shall in no event be held liable for any loss or other damages, including but not limited to special, incidental, consequential, or other damages. If you have any questions or concerns, the advice of a competent professional should be sought.

Manufactured in the United States of America.

ISBN: 978-1-62865-160-7

CONTENTS

DEDICATION

After two decades working in the media, where we tend to see and hear only the saddest, most awful and most depressing stories, I wanted to do something different with this book. I still firmly believe that nothing is more true, more defining and more common to the American spirit than our generosity, our kindness and our desire to help our fellow men and women. To that end, I am personally donating a portion of the proceeds from the sale of this book sold to these three wonderful charitable organizations, whom I heartily endorse.

I hope that everyone who purchases this book will also take the time to visit the websites of these very special organizations and learn more about the incredible work they do. It is also my hope that everyone who visits will consider making a pledge of further support for them. A little bit can go a long way, and together we can solve huge challenges that can often seem insurmountable.

Covenant House is the largest privately funded agency in the United States providing shelter and services that support runaway, homeless, and trafficked youth to move toward safe, stable, and loving places in their lives. It's mission is to serve suffering children of the street, and to protect and safeguard all children with absolute respect and unconditional love. Covenant House oversees 21 affiliates in the US, Canada, and Central America, serving approximately 60,000 homeless youth each year (including a potential 13,000 trafficked and sexually exploited youth, based on recent studies examining the possible link between human trafficking and youth homelessness). www. covenanthouse.org

Homes For Heroes is a private, voluntary, not-for-profit 501(c) (3) corporation. Its mission is to provide safe, dignified and supportive housing for honorably discharged men and women Veterans of U.S. Armed Forces, our wounded warriors who have been disabled or displaced by physical or mental wounds acquired in the millitary service of the United States of America. http://www.rocklandhomesforheroes.org/

People to People, NY's largest food pantry, helps feed the hungry by providing more than 1,200 families with groceries, produce, bread, dairy, meat and/or poultry products every month. In addition, People to People works to help an ever-increasing number of struggling Rocklanders through difficult times with dignity by providing clothing, school supplies, holiday gifts and other support. The single mother, the senior citizen, the veteran who comes to People to People – they all could be someone you know. Life's circumstances can change quickly – the loss of a job, the sudden death of a spouse, a tragic accident – and can cause a drastic change in one's ability to put food on the table and make ends meet. http://www.peopletopeopleinc.org/

FORWARD

I first spoke with Peter Danish earlier this year and immediately sensed a kindred spirit. He had written a particularly engaging book proposal for his new book, "I'll Give You Exactly Five Minutes". I was taken by the fact that although he already had a firm offer on the book, he continued to seek out what he considered the right publisher for the work – the right fit. In an hour-long conversation, he asked questions upon questions about Motivational Press and about me. It struck me immediately that he was the real deal, a professional's professional who wasn't afraid to admit he didn't have all the answers and was hoping to learn from me (despite the fact that I was some two decades his junior!) When we discussed his motivation for writing the book, his reply was interesting. He initially had no plan to write the book at all, but when client after client told him: "you really should write a book," he began to think they may have something. Despite the fact that his clientele was largely C-level executives and senior sales professionals, he really wanted to write a book that could apply to "everyman," particularly what he calls his "fellow sufferers."

You see, Mr. Danish is one of those millions of professionals who would rather have root-canal work without anesthesia than give a presentation. He detailed to me how over the years he has managed to contain and control his presentation anxiety, and put the energy to work for him. His goal was to share the information he'd culled together from 25 years of speech writing and speech-coaching. His hope was to providing help to those like him that suffered the tortures of the damned before getting up to deliver a speech or a presentation.

When I asked him how long it took him to write the book, he said: "*25 years. The book and the system represent the combined wisdom of quite literally hundreds of colleagues and clients and thousands of presentations.*" But it was more than just a compilation of "best practices of CEOs," it was theory and formula that was born of thousands of hours of observation, and distilled into a simple, user-friendly system. He had not created a rule book or a series of tips, tricks and secrets – because he doesn't believe any of those things provide meaningful, lasting improvement. Rather, in a delightfully anecdotal style, Mr. Danish shows readers how to help themselves by providing a cogent, highly accessible framework that they can apply to their own situations.

His emphasis on just a few simple, central themes, "*honesty, clarity and passion,*" was a real breath of fresh air in an industry cluttered with mountains of short-cuts, gimmick and tricks. As a writer and entrepreneur who is constantly looking to improve myself every day, I was especially please to read that this book never claims to have all the answers, or to be an end in and of itself. Instead, it speaks of the journey of self-improvement and the daily discipline required to achieve meaningful and lasting improvement. I found myself smiling, nodding my head and often laughing out loud at the stories contained in the book, but by the end I realized this is a book that everyone can benefit from.

Justin Sachs

PREFACE

I was on the phone with the representative from a major publisher of business books discussing "I'll Give You Exactly Five Minutes" when I was struck by an incredible irony. The publisher was telling me that he enjoyed the book and how I had found a niche, yada yada yada. However, the purpose of the phone call was to inform me that my book was in fact too short! In order to make it profitable in any meaningful sense, we would have to charge nearly double what I had recommended as the selling price.

His solution was simple: make it longer. Write more. Put in some more background charts, some statistics, and illustrations. Add other funny anecdotes about experiences with clueless CEOs *(his words, not mine)*. In short: add filler. Fluff it up. No one will notice.

See the irony? The whole point of the book is brevity and succinctness and the publisher is recommending "fluffing it up just a bit." The title of the book itself talks about cutting to the chase and yet the publisher wanted to add filler.

I understood the economics of the situation, but could not see my way clearly to fattening up a book about cutting out the fat just to make the profit margin more acceptable to the publisher.

I didn't write this book for the benefit of publishers or printers. I wrote it in the hope that it can help, even in a small way, folks like me who are not natural-born speakers; I want it to help people who don't like the spotlight, and those who would rather have major dental work than give a speech.

I also wanted to de-bunk some of the bad presentation-giving advice that is out there masquerading as expertise. In my own personal quest to improve my skills, I have read dozens of books on improving my presentation skills and I can say, without exception, that virtually none of them helped me at all. To quantify it, in researching this book, I read over thirty very well reviewed books on improving presentation skills. To my dismay, very few of them had anything really substantive to offer in terms of actionable, practical, "boots on the ground" advice, either. I found myself getting frustrated, and over and over again saying: "Well, that's just stupid."

The vast majority of the "expertise" was simply innocuous and instantly forgettable ("just be yourself"). But, some of it, I found to be more than just bad advice - it was downright crazy, and would certainly do more damage than good. It motivated me to write this book.

We live in an era when the ability to stand before an audience and deliver an impactful presentation is an increasingly valuable, if not critical, commodity. Despite the digital revolution, teleconferences, video conferences, Skype, webmeetings, webcasts, etc., nothing has replaced face to face communication as the single most powerful and persuasive communication tool that we have.

Over the last quarter century, I have been lucky enough to have worked with some incredibly talented speakers and presenters, ranging from C-Level Executives to Sales persons to Actors, and I have compiled and organized some of the very best practices from the best of those presenters into a simple system. It is an evolutionary system, not a revolutionary one. It will not shake the earth around you, or be a life-changing experience. It will help you *immediately* with your next presentation.

The goal is to find your own style, to adapt these principles and make them your own, rather than force a rigid set of rules onto your natural style. That will allow you to interact and engage with your audiences with increased ease, poise, and confidence. It will ultimately help deliver your message in a clear, concise, and meaningful manner.

Perhaps most importantly, I want to stress that this book is not an end in and of itself; it's only a beginning. It is designed to help you continue to improve your skills long after this book is gathering dust on your shelf; it will provide the tools, the technique, and the confidence to maintain your progress throughout the rest of your career.

It is not a complex set of theories, it is manual of easily adaptable techniques and useful solutions. I set out to make the book available to as many people as possible. In order to do that, I decided that I'd have to price it at a point that is affordable to anyone; luckily, I found an ideal publisher in Motivational Press. Their corporate philosopy was music to my ears and the support that they have provided has been nothing short of inspirational.

After reading "I'll Give You Exactly 5 Minutes!" it is my sincere hope that you will emerge a better prepared and more confident speaker in any situation. To that end, please feel free to reach out and contact me with your thoughts.

Good luck and good reading!

Peter Danish

PROLOGUE

The myth of "speech coaching" and "public speaking" books, seminars, and courses

Did you know?

As of this printing, Amazon.com currently lists 41,505 titles on "public speaking" and another 17,000 on "Improving your presentation skills." This means that there are currently over 60,000 people in the United States who think themselves expert enough to have written books on how to improve your skills. If you ask me, that is a lot of experts. If you try to think of all the people you've seen present or give a speech in your entire lifetime, I will bet that you could only come up with a handful that you really thought were "experts."

Gimme a break! It has been my observation that the average sales person, men and women who have to sell every single day, have forgotten more about presenting than these so-called experts will ever know. However, sometimes they just need to tap into that knowledge in a more formalized fashion.

Guess what?

Of those 60 thousand books, 99.999% of them will not help you at all. (Henceforth we will refer to those books simply as "the 99%"). That is not to say that they are not well meaning, as I am sure that they are. That is not to say that they all contain nothing that will help you whatsoever; some have wonderful techniques, tips, and tricks. However, most do not. They set the bar very low. Most contain tired, stale, and archaic drivel that should have left the business lexicon years ago.

Here is an inconvenient truth: some people are just not good presenters and no amount of books, online courses, or seminars at the local Holiday Inn are going to turn them into Steve Jobs. Sorry, but it needed to be said.

How do I know this?

I have been speech-coaching C-level execs and writing hundreds of sales presentations for blue chip clients for over 20 years. My career has largely been spent helping people communicate, whether it be a sales person, a middle-manager or a C-level executive. I've worked with presenters of all shapes and sizes – men, women and children – in large groups, small groups and individually. Or, as I like to say: "the good, the bad, and the ugly."

During that time, I've written countless speeches, PSAs, corporate communications, and sales presentations. I have massaged talking points and corrected body language to the point that I should have a chiropractic degree by now. I have pointed out millions of bad mannerisms, distracting gestures, and employed enough best practices to make my old G.E. Six Sigma teachers proud.

After all this, I have arrived at one universal truth:

Action Point:
There is no "right way" to present.

And, if anyone ever tells you there is, run away from them – fast! Even if they have tons of empirical data to support them, trust me – there is an equal amount of evidence to contradict them.

I love the composers Wagner and Strauss; my wife says they are like nails on the blackboard. No two people see the same images, hear the same sounds, and process sensory input the same way. And, for the millions of permutations, there are as many sub-permutations based on taste. What works for one will never ever be guaranteed to work for another. It's human nature.

Here's your first exercise:

Try to think of the best presenters you have ever seen. Come up with a list of 3-5 of them. Then, give some thought to what all of their styles of presentation had in common.

I predict that you will discover one thing that they all have in common: they have nothing in common. This is particularly obvious on a physical level. Each will have his/her own posture, speech pattern, hand gestures, cadence, and body language.

What do all these people with nothing in common have in common? Look at the previous paragraph and the one common denominator in every item is "his/her own."

ACTION POINT:

Many of the greatest speakers of all time didn't follow the rules.
The best continue not to.

Second Exercise: TED vs. C-SPAN

Watch some of the speakers at the annual TED conference (you can find them all on YouTube) and you will notice a vast diversity of styles, almost all of them riveting in their own way. Then, turn on C-span for a few minutes (but not too much longer – you might fall asleep) and watch several speakers. Then, compare the speakers from the TED conference with the speakers on Capitol Hill. The difference will be staggering. The first thing that you will immediately notice (even with the sound off) is the body language. Then, you will notice the style of speaking. Finally, the dramatically different use of gestures.

You know what you will likely conclude very quickly? Even the worst speaker at the TED conference is more interesting than the best politician. Why do you think that is?

I did this exact exercise with ten college students recently. I showed them about a half hour of each network randomly picking the speakers. The students were astonished to see how "wooden," "stiff," and "phoney" the politicians appeared after watching the TED presenters. I asked them to write down the three words that best described each speaker.

TED Results: "Awesome," "Brilliant," "Authentic," "Honest."

The C-Span Results: "Stiff," "Wooden," "Boring," "Phoney."

The two words used most often were "honest" and "phoney."

What does that tell us?

You can watch hundreds of different presenters, one after another, and observe that no two are similar. There will be commonalities, that's natural, but the most memorable, entertaining, and effective ones by far are always the ones you perceive to be most personally authentic and most passionate about their material: honest.

ACTION POINT:
At the end of the day, honesty and passion trump form and technique every time.

And, the very best news is that honesty and passion are things you bring to the table. They are about the material, but they are more than just the words that you use and the information that you share. They are not learned from a book, a course, or a self-help guru. They are the immutable elements that establish a bond of trust between speaker and audience. That bond, that sense of communion with the audience, is where credibility is born.

Another incomprehensible truth about presentation skills books:

As hard to believe as it may seem, you can go through dozens and dozens of books on improving your speaking and presentation skills without ever finding the word "honest." In my professional opinion, "honesty" is the Holy Grail of presenting – nothing else is as important or as irreplaceable.

Don't worry about being an eloquent speaker: be real, authentic, and honest. People prefer honesty. People respect honesty. People trust honesty. Honesty is the essential element in making all of our interactions more meaningful and productive.

ACTION POINT:
Eloquence without honesty is mere decoration

There's no shame in being a poor presenter.

However, being poorly prepared is another story. Chances are, if you are reading this book, you have already had extensive experience in public speaking, delivering sales presentations, corporate communications, or another like field. Chances are, as well, that this is not the first book that you've read in your quest to improve your presentation skills. It is not easy: if it were, everyone would be good at it. Also, as I stated earlier, there is no single correct answer for everyone, no one-size-fits-all. You are going to have to try on a few hats to find the one that fits you the best.

First, let me say that this is not a book designed for 60 minute keynote addresses. It is a highly personalized and practical application of a tried and tested technique; it also includes suggestions for the average presenter looking to get better, stress out a little bit less, and ultimately feel a bit better about their next presentation. That is not to say the technique does not apply to the Fortune 500 CEO as well, because it does. Moreover, it is a simple and direct system assembled from vast experience and designed to help you immediately.

These aren't abstract, philosophical concepts, but rather, direct, applicable, "boots-on-the-ground" practical techniques and tips that will make your professional life easier. Simply put, do not expect me to tell you how many bullets to put on your PowerPoint slides, or what color tie to wear.

It's a lonely job.

So what's the bottom line? Some people are born presenters – most are not. If you are not, you will never ever be a natural. You'll have to work at it – hard and often.

If you are *not* one of the blessed few who loves to be in front of people, and has a natural gift for connecting with an audience – congratulations! You are one of the millions of business professionals who would rather eat glass than give a presentation.

This book is for you. I decided to put these thoughts on paper because, in the last year, three different CEOs from major media companies told me: "you really ought to write a book."

I am a firm believer in that, if a company hires you year after year to speech coach them, you are simply not being hard enough on them. Nobody likes being told their baby is ugly, it's human nature. So, there has to be a balancing act on the part of the coach: equal parts honey and vinegar, because here is a little secret:

> *Every successful business person thinks they are a good presenter! And every __really__ successful business person thinks they are a __really__ good presenter.*

Sometimes, they are right. Often, they are not. The coach has to do the dance that he or she thinks will elicit the best out of each one. That means he/she has to be able to listen to a lot of pontificating (e.g. "Do you have any idea how many presentations I give each year?" "I was a keynote speaker when you were still in diapers," and "Excuse me, I earned 600 thousand dollars last year. How much did you make?").

Another of the situations that I have grown weary of is when an executive tells me that he wants complete candor and honesty about his or her skills: "I want you to give it to me straight! Don't pull punches. Be brutal." Most of the time, what they actually want to hear is: "I love it! It's perfect! Don't change a thing!" And then, your first critical word is met with an avalanche of indignation and defensive posturing.

A good coach must have the confidence and gravitas to tell a high-powered executive or a captain of industry that they are wrong about something, and hold their ground firmly. They must be able to say: "That joke is not funny," "that anecdote is too long," or "you need to cut five minutes or you're going to put everyone to sleep." Or: "you really need to rehearse this some more." The trick is to be able to do it without ruffling too many feathers and bruising too many egos. Constructive criticism is a nice concept, but no matter how constructive it is, it's rarely well received. At the end of the day, in order to be most effective, it must be more than simply constructive criticism – it must be compassionate criticism. Compassionate criticism engages the intuitive mind of the presenter and focuses solely on finding the value in every word, every gesture, every movement; keeping the energy positive at all times, which almost invariably promotes openness, generates good energy, and ultimately enhances the results. And, even if it doesn't always take you all the way from A to Z, it will at least help develop a logical framework for the presenter to get there and to better define precisely what it is he or she wants to say.

In addition to my corporate work, I have worked or consulted for several New York dramatic arts conservatories. Working with the gifted acting teachers there has taught me more about effective communications and presenting than the hundreds of books and dozens of seminars I have read or attended over the last two decades (I will go into the details shortly). Compassionate criticism is something I learned at a conservatory watching the acting teachers working with young actors. Finding and noting every possible positive aspect about a performance before moving to the challenges. The fundamental difference between the young actors and the average presenter is that the young actors really really want to get better at their craft.

ACTION POINT:
You really have to <u>want</u> to get better.

This sounds so simple that it's almost ridiculous and yet it remains one of the biggest stumbling blocks I come across. Improving any skill can be a humbling process especially presentation skill because generally the persons called upon to give the most presentations are often not particularly humble. (Sorry, but it's true.) To really improve in a meaningful way, one needs to let go and expose a part of themselves and having to do that makes a lot of people uncomfortable.

ACTION POINT:
You must learn to drop your shields (the Dangers of Defense)

It's another lesson that sounds easy but it's one of the very hardest to learn and one of the biggest energy drains I encounter on a regular basis: defensiveness in the presenter. Of course, it's only human nature, and to a degree, it is completely involuntary – nonetheless, it is a major impediment. Nobody likes being told they are wrong, and even fewer like being proven wrong. So, our defensive nature throws up a protective shield from any anxiety that might accompany having our shortcomings revealed. But, until you can let it go and commit 100% to improvement, you will always have a handicap. We will work on this later in the book and develop techniques to deal with it. Once you see how much faster you improve after you've dropped your shields, you will never raise them again (at least not consciously).

As I mentioned in the forward, I decided to make this book available to as wide an audience as possible at a price that anyone can afford. The reason for this altruism is simple: **I am a fellow sufferer.**

I have panic attacks before presentations, sweat like an animal in heat during presentations, and beat myself up mercilessly after presentations. This book is for you fellow sufferers. If it can help alleviate even some of the suffering you go through and elevate your performance just a bit, then I will consider my work done. It is not 500 pages; in fact, it's barely 100 pages, specifically because I believe in practicing what I preach.

I've tried to present all the material contained here in the most user-friendly, plain language possible. I have always found that excessively intricate and complicated language creates a barrier between author and reader, so there will be no clinical or antiseptic language here (irony intended). Nor will the material be soaked in any touchy-feely, self-help, new age nonsense.

My system is simple, direct, and concise (as all good presentations should be), and can be applied to virtually any scenario, from keynote speaking to large audiences, to sales presentations to small audiences, to one-on-one interviews.

Because no matter what the occasion, each of these scenarios at their core, have two basic but critical goals in common:

1. Provide the audience with the proper information.

2. Persuade the audience to come to the proper conclusion

Everything else is just gravy.

CHAPTER ONE: THE POWER OF BAD ADVICE

**I guarantee you that the stupidest advice you will
ever receive will come from a speech coach.**

A history and a culture of bad advice.

Reading through dozens and dozens of books on public speaking, patterns begin to emerge. After a while, they *all* look and sound the same. They have much in common, and more importantly, they all tend to share some very bad suggestions. Here, we will look at a couple of classic examples of incomprehensibly stupid advice. In the interest of brevity, and because I respect your intelligence, I will not use extended anecdotes to illustrate every item; I'm sure you will get the point.

"Don't *over* rehearse.   Once you've got it, stop."

Guess what? There is no such thing as over rehearsing. Just because your early passes at a speech or presentation were better than the later ones doesn't mean you are over rehearsed. 99 times out of 100, you were not as ready as you thought you were, and the early passes were smoother because you were more relaxed and not over thinking everything.

ACTION POINT:
There is no such thing as over rehearsing.

Truth? Practice really does make perfect. And more practice makes more perfect.

A few years ago, my good friend actress Rita Harvey was starring on Broadway in the new production of "Fiddler on the Roof." She received her script over a month before the first rehearsal. She spent that month committing virtually the entire show – almost every role – to memory. This was before the first rehearsal. They began rehearsals three months before the show was to open. Then, they had two weeks of previews. Then, when the show finally opened, the general consensus among the cast was that it was a good two to three weeks into the run before they really hit their stride.

Let us recap: one month of preparation, three months of rehearsal every day, two weeks of previews - and it still took two weeks of performances (eight per week) - before they felt they had hit their stride. And, when they performed it, it looked fresh as a daisy every night.

"It usually takes me more than three weeks to prepare a good impromptu speech."

- Mark Twain

Here's another great example:

I went to see Paul McCartney in concert a few years ago at Madison Square Garden. As he prepared to play a song at the piano, he paused and very matter-of-factly told the audience:

"This song... well, I gotta tell you a funny story that happened to me earlier today, and it relates to this song."

He then proceeded to tell a hilarious off-hand anecdote about getting a massage at the hotel earlier in the day from a masseuse that spoke no English. The fellow had no idea whom he was rubbing down – or, so Paul thought – until the masseuse started humming "The Long and Winding Road."

The audience went wild and Paul ended saying: *"True story! Happened just this afternoon!"* Then, he launched into a beautiful rendition of "The Long and Winding Road."

His ability to tell a funny story, with seemingly no preparation at all, was amazing. The story was cute, endearing, and total *bullshit*.

The following week, I saw his concert again in Boston, and he told the exact same story, word for word. The audience went wild again. Then, six months later, I saw him in a stadium in Los Angeles and guess what? That's right - the same story.

Did I feel cheated? Maybe just a little. But as a presentation coach, I felt that I was being schooled by a master. I took the trouble to speak to several friends who were stage hands at the Meadowlands arena, and they told me that he did the entire story during rehearsal and at sound check earlier in the day. He managed day after day to find something in the story to keep it like new for him, and consequently, it felt fresh for his audience. As the great violinist Jascha Heifitz said:

"If I don't practice one day, I know it. If I don't practice two days, my critics know it. If I don't practice three days, everyone knows it."

The greatest of the greats rehearse the most. See my point? Over rehearse? No such thing.

ACTION POINT:
The more you rehearse, the less you look "rehearsed."

How do you know when you have rehearsed enough? There is no absolute answer, but I like to suggest rehearsing it to the point that you have "almost" memorized it. Do not aim to memorize it, but simply *almost* memorize it. Like a great musician who practices his scales till they are second nature, then throws them away and riffs on them, you should know the material so well that you can riff on it as well.

> *"I'm sorry for the long length of this letter, but I didn't have time to write a shorter one."*
>
> *- George Bernard Shaw*

Periodically throughout the book, I will be dropping in some classic examples of bad advice. I do this partly for entertainment purposes (let's face it – some of it is funny), but to illustrate just how harmful a lot of presentation coaching really can be.

Ten Very Good Examples of Very Bad Advice

(No particular order.)

1. **Just be yourself, and you will be fine.**

   a. If you are a charming and dynamic personality, this is great. But, what if you're a bookish nerd and you know it? Then what?

2. **Visualize a successful outcome and you will have one.**

   a. And, if you're good, Santa will leave you a present. This is fantasy. Your time would be better spent reviewing data and immersing yourself in the material.

3. **Provide more data than you need to make your point.**

   a. Too much data is one of the surest cures for insomnia.

   b. When was the last time you heard someone complain that a speech was too short? The right anwer is 'never.'

4. Distribute handouts *before* you speak so the audience can read along *with* the speaker.

    a. Yes, and *ahead* of the speaker. Never show your cards in advance, you will lose all the drama of the story unfolding.

    b. If you must have handouts, save them for takeaways or appendices at the end.

5. Use Props and Visual Aids.

    a. Nothing in the world compromises the integrity of a speaker, and by extension, his speech, than the use of a prop.

    b. It screams out to the audience that either the material is not strong enough to stand on its own two feet, or the presenter isn't. Or, the unspoken third possibility is that the speaker thinks the audience is not smart enough to get his or her point without help.

6. Plant your feet shoulder width apart for maximum stability.

    a. Rigid is bad; it is stressful and not relaxed. You do not need stability, you need flexibility. Movement means comfort.

7. When your mouth dries out, lightly bite your tongue to get the saliva flowing.

    a. Don't get me started: So many things can go wrong, I cannot begin to list them.

8. Picture the audience naked.

    a. If you pictured some of the members of your audiences naked, you would be traumatized. Forget this idea: it's a distraction, and anything that draws your attention away from the material is bad.

9. Practice your speech in front of a mirror.

    a. Have you ever tried this? It can be a disaster. Again, it is a distraction. It is impossible to focus on your material and not be distracted by your image.

10. With practice, you can develop charisma.

    a. This is pure fiction: with practice you can develop confidence. Charisma comes from God, not a speech coach.

"But, Peter," you say, "these books have been extremely useful to me! They have pointed out my bad style and bad mannerisms and bad posture! And, I have learned that I am doing all kinds of things wrong as well. I am terrible!" Says who? These 60,000+ so called experts? Forget them! There is a harsh truth here.

ACTION POINT:

Presentation training can actually do a lot more harm than good.

Anyone who has read more than one book on improving presentation skills, or attended one seminar or class, can tell you that more often than not, you actually feel far less natural and authentic than you did before. That is completely antithetical to good communication. All of the correct postures, dramatic gestures, and clever speech inflections in the world are not going to make you sound one bit more honest or authentic in your presentation.

CHAPTER TWO: STRUCTURE

The ORSON System: The absolute simplest structure that you have ever seen; it will be the best that you have ever tried.

"If <u>you</u> don't know what you want to achieve in your presentation your audience never will."

- Harvey Diamond

I began to develop the ORSON System about ten years ago, and I have used it in every presentation and speech that I've written or coached since. I have also used it in job interviews, radio and press interviews, and news conferences. Like most other inventions, it was born of necessity. In this particular case, the CEO of a brand new cable network was preparing for his first Network Upfront Presentation. For those not in the media business, the network upfronts are major dog-and-pony shows that the networks do in the Spring of each year, in which they roll out their new Fall programming and then ask advertisers to give them their money a year in advance (or Upfront) in exchange for a discounted rate on large blocks of media. This CEO actually had one hundred pages of notes for his speech. I had neither the time nor the inclination to search through them hoping to find some tidbits of information on which to construct his speech.

I wrote out a very simple chart for him (not dissimilar to the chart on the next page) and told him "distill, edit, condense." At first, he laughed and said it wasn't possible. But, the following day, he emailed me the chart back; it was filled out. And so we began and so the ORSON System was born.

> *"If you don't know where you are going, you'll end up someplace else."*
>
> *- Yogi Berra*

(**Author's note**: For years people have poked fun at Yogi Berra and his "Yogisms" for his simplicity and his apparent self-contradictions, but take a look at some of his wisdom and I think that you will find he was one of the great minds of our time.)

Elementary

Every good presentation contains four elements. We will talk about each one briefly:

- **Structure**: Structure provides guidance and improves clarity and flow of the presentation. The ORSON System will help you develop your structure. The old adage that "every speech must have a logical beginning, middle, and end" will melt away. It will be replaced by a new sequence that the audience will always be able to follow, and no speaker should be able to forget.

- **Content**: A speech or interview is a one-time, real-time affair. Your audience will absorb it instantaneously as you deliver it. There are no do-overs or re-takes, so the content has to be crystal clear and compelling the first time, and every time, you mention it. To capture the ever-shrinking attention of the distracted executive, the content must provide valuable, concise insights relevant to the challenges that your audience is facing. It is the meat and potatoes – before you pour on the gravy.

- **Packaging**: Packaging is the gravy, the elements of style. It is the preparation and the delivery system. Developing the packaging is a painstaking process and will often vary from one audience to the next because it is the most audience-centric element of your presentation. It is everything from clothes to posture, and so on.

- **Passion**: Passion is the fuel of persuasion. The one element that makes or breaks most presentations is the passion with which it is delivered. It is the human element. Whereas the structure, content, and packaging are inanimate, the passion is the one element that you have total control of.

These elements must independently and collaboratively serve two simple functions:

1. Provide the audience with the proper information.
2. Persuade the audience to come to the desired conclusion.

Define Your Purpose

Perhaps you have heard the expression: begin with the end in mind? Well, to effectively achieve these two functions, the first steps every single presentation, interview, or speech should begin with are very basic and fundamental questions. In simple terms, describe the specific things you want your audience:

1. to think,
2. to remember,
3. and ultimately, to do.

Throughout the course of this book, you will be asked regularly to refer to these answers.

Here is a brief time line for your presentation structure:

00-1:00 **OVERVIEW**: Here's the deal.

There is a problem/a need/a challenge…

1:00-02:00 **RESEARCH:** How do I know?

Dazzle them with knowledge /data/metrics

2:00-4:00 **SOLUTION:** But what can we do about it?

No problems – only solutions! This is how we fix it.

4:00-5:00 **OPPORTUNITY**: Here's what it means to you.

This is the "why" we are doing it. The financial angle.

5:00 **NEXT STEPS**: So, where do we go from here?

Five minutes, no more. Yikes, that was simple! Who knew?

Now let's breakdown each section and analyze each in a bit more detail:

Overview:

Ask yourself this question: *"What exactly is the problem/the need/the challenge?"* Your Overview will answer that question. The problem is:

_____.

One great way to really engage your audience is through a challenge or a prediction.

(I predict that before I leave here today, you will….)

In addition to capturing their attention, it immediately makes the listener a participant. He or she goes from being passively to actively engaged. Another simple way to immediately engage your audience is by asking for a show of hands in response to a question. If you are in a group setting, asking a question that begins with: "How many of you knew that...?" will invariably get people sitting up and looking around to see how everyone else voted.

Always keep your Overview brief and directly to the point. Of course, your audience is interested in you and wants to hear about you, but they are actually far more interested in getting to the point – quickly. A clear, concise overview is always preferable to a questionable joke or a longwinded list of your accomplishments.

Here is my favorite overview. It comes from Scott Cook, founder of Intuit (makers of Quicken and Turbo Tax):

> *"How many of you balance your checkbooks? (every hand went up) How many of you like doing it? (every hand went down) You're not alone. Millions of people around the world also hate balancing their check books. My company, Intuit, has developed a very simple, easy-to-use personal finance tool that we call Quicken. We are confident that many people around the world who hate balancing their check book will want to buy Quicken."*
>
> *Absolute Perfection in 30 seconds.*

Research:

Once again ask yourself: *"And just how do I know this?"* Your Research will answer that question. This is your big moment to show them how smart you are, and that you know your information. That does not give you a license to go into information overload: there is a big difference between burying an audience with data, and dazzling and persuading them with thoughtful knowledge and keen insight.

Two easy things you want to accomplish here are:

- Establish your credibility by identifying your position, knowledge of the current situation, expertise, and qualifications.

- Communicate the crying need to change the status quo.

Do not get bogged down by over-explaining technology, process, or models. You do not need to provide sophisticated statistical analysis and mathematical modeling at this point – a few well placed statistics and facts are far more impactful than a massive data dump. Move on, and be concise.

Solution:

Q: *"So how do we fix this?"* Answer this question with your solution. This is the meat and potatoes of any presentation and it can't afford any fat. It needs to be lean and to the point. You have already identified the problem and you've shown them that you understand the depth of the issues surrounding it. Now, be brilliant and explain how you are going to get it done. Whether the solution is strategic, tactical, organizational, or process improvement, you should differentiate your plan immediately and stick to why it is different, how it is better: reinforce the untenability of the status quo along the way.

Keep it slow and steady. Use simple language and short punchy sentences. Pause periodically to let strong ideas sink in. Your audience needs time to absorb and take breaks, too.

Opportunity:

Q: *If we fix the problem, what will be the benefits?* Answer this question and do not shy away from using figures: they quantify and add authenticity to your big payoff. Encapsulate the idea and the opportunity.

When framing the Opportunity portion of your presentation, bare in mind one technical direction:

The fear of loss is always a greater motivational force than the possibility of gain. The same opportunity framed differently has a significant effect on consumer behavior. It is completely irrational behavior, but economists have studied it for years and concluded that people in general strongly prefer to avoid possible loss rather than acquire gains.

Once again, to the extent possible, stick to simple, precise language and go easy on the technical jargon. Be sure once again to reinforce the risk or danger of the status quo, and be clear on the benefits: list and quantify them.

Next Steps:

Q: *"So where do we go from here?"* Destination. This is where you want to arrive. Encourage questions. Discuss next steps and assign specific responsibilities for action.

ACTION POINT:

Once you have hit on all your critical points of focus, all anxiety will disappear and your confidence will shine.

Here is a cheat sheet you can use to build your next presentation. You, no doubt, noticed that the five-step system that I have laid out and discussed creates an acronym. I call it ORSON, or the ORSON system. I suggest you retype it yourself and save it. Then, you can print out multiple copies for future use, because once you try it, you're going to love it.

1. **O**verview – state the issue.

2. **R**esearch – show you know your stuff.

3. **S**olution – here is how we fix it.

4. **O**pportunity – the big payoff of the fix.

5. **N**ext Steps – where do we go from here?

Wait! That's it? That's all there is? Why, yes. As you will no doubt realize by the end of this book, I am a big fan of acronyms. I use them daily to help remember lists. I have taught virtually every presenter that I have coached the benefits of using them and using them often.

Now, we have our first simple exercise. I want you to think of a recent presentation that you have given, or are about to give. Then, on a pad of paper, I want you to draw a line down the center and jot down the ORSON elements in the left column. Then, in the right column, jot down the corresponding real life information from you presentation.

The first time you do it, you may get a little bit bogged down trying to find the exact words for each element, but do not stress over it. The exact words are not critical; it's the concept that is important. I have deliberately chosen very broad stroke concepts:

Overview|**R**esearch|**S**olution|**O**pportunity|**N**ext steps

---

The reason for this is specifically that you don't get stuck on exact words; so that you can trigger the idea in your memory and then riff on it. This will add an element of complete freshness, honesty, and authenticity to your presentation.

It should not take more than a minute or two, and it will add a mile-high perspective to your presentation.

ORSON Worksheet

1. Overview: the problem/need/challenge.

   _____

   _____

2. Research: the data/proof/support.

   _____

   _____

3. Solution: the fix.

   _____

   _____

4. Opportunity: the big payoff of the fix.

   _____

   _____

5. Next Steps: where do we go from here?

   _____

   _____

If you find that you do not have room to write out your notes on this worksheet, think about editing them down. Remember, this worksheet is designed for broad-stroke concepts, not exact words. Look at the answers to the questions that we asked in the previous chapter once again, and understand the essence of each point in just a few words. Once again, this acronym is only meant to trigger your memory of the five parts of your presentation. Technical mastery of the system will come quickly once you begin to recognize and get comfortable with the linear logic of the system. And the broad-stroke nature of the "triggers" will give you far more freedom to create and invent within the structure.

I reiterate my musical analogy:

Practice your scales till they are second nature – then forget about them and riff.

Try it a few times with sample presentations. Do not worry about specifics. You will find very quickly that you can easily remember the five basic points you wish to get across.

Once you feel comfortable with the technique – and you will in no time at all – try applying the simple principles to several different situations.

First, explore its use in a simple five minute public address. Then, use it again to create a five minute sales presentation. Next, use the technique in a sample job interview scenario. You will find that with just a little bit of practice, the simple acronym ORSON will free you from your reliance on scripts, outlines, index cards and so on. The simple breakdown and organization of your material into these five simple sections will make your life much easier.

I have shared this simple acronym with numerous C-Level Executives, and I watch with pride when I see them use it even when they are not giving a speech or major presentation – instances such as TV interviews, sales meetings, etc.

All you need to memorize is one word: ORSON.

> *"If you don't know what you want to achieve in your presentation your audience never will."*
>
> *- Harvey Diamond*

CHAPTER THREE: Content Part One:

Good B.S. and Bad B.S.

You mean to tell me there's actually such a thing as good B.S.?

Brevity and Simplicity

How important is brevity? No one in recorded history has ever uttered the words: "I wish that presentation ran a bit longer." In fact, several of the greatest thinkers have had something to say on the subject of brevity:

> *"Life is really simple, but we insist on making it complicated."*
>
> *-Confucius*

> *"Simplicity is the ultimate sophistication."*
>
> *- Leonardo da Vinci*

> *"There's no greatness where there is not simplicity, goodness and truth."*
>
> *- Leo Tolstoy*

> *"Nature is pleased with simplicity. And nature is no dummy"*
>
> *- Isaac Newton*

Is that enough? Do you believe me now?   In a more practical application, here is the greatest sales pitch in history and possibly the shortest (don't blink, you might miss it):

"Jaws in Space."

When Ridley Scott's producers for the film "Alien" went looking for financing, their entire sales pitch was exactly three words: Jaws in Space. It was short, to the point, and it completely conveyed everything the producer needed to say. In a word: brilliant.

That is the gold standard, and it only happens a couple of times in a career – if you are lucky. But, that model is a very efficient and effective one.

That leads us to the place where we begin to discuss content. Remember, ORSON is a system of organizing your content in the simplest and most efficient fashion for clear, concise, and entertaining presentations. But, before you even begin, write down these five questions and jot down very brief answers. Those answers are your building blocks; they will start you on your quest for quality content.

1. What is your ultimate goal?
2. What is the single most important piece of information that you want every audience member to take away from your presentation?
3. If you had to condense your presentation into 30 words, what would they be?
4. What are your three pillars of wisdom?

Once you have answered these questions begin to outline your content. Creating an outline will give your content shape, flow and coherence.

Think back to your Overview, your "problem/challenge/need;" it is likely your hook, and everything should relate back to that hook.

Simplicity

There are conflicting schools of thought about how much information the human brain can absorb and digest in a given time. Consequently, there are varying theories about how many points you should attempt to get across in a speech or presentation. Your audience spends its days in a perpetual state of information overload. That is exactly why simplicity is so critical, and so powerful.

If you pack too much information into the presentation, you will overwhelm people and drastically reduce the likelihood that your message will come across, let alone be remembered: so keep it simple.

Earlier, I asked you to think back and try to remember some of the best presenters that you could remember. I bet that you will find the finest were the ones who could distill complex thoughts and concepts into simple, memorable words that their audience could grasp immediately and retain.

The Power of Three

Based on no science whatsoever – other than having worked on hundreds of presentations – I have arrived at the conclusion that the magic number is actually three.

Several years ago, while working on an Upfront presentation for a major television network, I was on a plane headed home to New York from Miami when I received a copy of the script for the show. As I read it, I was feeling a bit overwhelmed. First of all it was long – very long.

ACTION POINT:
Long = Boring. Boring = Death.

Luckily, I was seated next to the Executive Vice President of Sales on the flight.   I asked him plainly: "Do you like this?"   He replied that it was certainly comprehensive and well written.   I asked him, "If you had your druthers, what would be the three things you would want every single person in attendance at the event to walk away with?" He told me, and I wrote them down.   Then, I asked him to find those three points in the current presentation.   He found two of them and they were 30 slides apart.

"Is that going to help you move the needle in sales?" I asked.   He got visibly annoyed and took out a pad and pencil, and said: "Let's re-write this thing right here, right now." We did so. And, by the time we were in New York, we had cut some 20 slides and 30 minutes from the presentation.   We focused solely on what we jokingly called our "Three Pillars of Wisdom," and made what was a ponderous epic into a taunt thriller.

There is an old adage that comes in many forms: "Try to please everybody and you'll wind up pleasing nobody." This is especially true in presenting.   A presentation that tries to be all things to everybody usually winds up being nothing to anyone.

You need to focus on what Six Sigma people call the CTQs, or *critical to quality* issues.   All of the points which you arrive at must help your audience arrive at the right decision; the easiest way to do that is always to help them understand that it is in their own best interest to follow your advice.   And, the surest was to make sure they do understand, is for you to craft the presentation from their point of view.   Continually ask: "What is in it for me?" and then structure your presentation around the answer to those questions.

I have personally attended over 50 television network upfront presentations, and it is shocking how many of them were really poorly done.   Virtually, every one of them have suffered from the TMI syndrome: too much information.   The producers always tried to throw in absolutely everything but the kitchen sink into their presentations.

Some looked remarkably beautiful, with no expense spared: live feeds from all around the globe, big stars performing, etc. But you came out of 99% of them able to remember almost nothing that you heard or saw in the presentation.

The Danger of the Digital Age

Our current age of hyper-high-speed data and continual information overload has had a very noticeable and crippling effect on the clarity and cohesiveness of presentations.

The Upfront that I was referring to took place over a decade ago, but I can still remember the three pillars perfectly clearly today (and the three pillars from the following year's presentation as well).

Don't Be Boring (Remember "honesty and passion")

Just kidding! That sounds like one of those pieces of bad advice that I advised you against since the beginning. Do not get bogged down with specific words or data. If you get stuck, move on. An audience will always forgive you for small stumbles if they sense it is coming from a place of honesty.

Some speech coaches recommend "catching" your audience with your intro. Have a great icebreaker. It is nice, but not critical. In all seriousness, it is not a total death sentence if you don't grab the audience's attention at the start. The real goal, and the greatest challenge, is not *getting* the audience's attention, it is *keeping* it.

Here is a baker's dozen facts to help develop compelling content:

1. **It's easier to make *things* that people *want* than to make people *want things*:** I sometimes refer to this as the Steve Jobs axiom. It reminds us that it is not about us; it is always about your audience. Fundamentally, when you try to make things people want, you are going over to join them. When you try to make people want things, you are forcing them to come over to you.

2. **The surest way to get people to do things with you is to join then in what they are already doing:** Today's audiences are busier and more stressed than ever. In short, no one has any time for anything anymore. So, make it easy for them. While preparing for your presentation, speech, or interview, remember to examine every point you wish to make both from your perspective (what you want to communicate) and from your audience's perspective (what you think they are expecting to hear or learn.)

Even in his last acceptance speech, President Obama understood the importance of keeping it all about the audience:

"Above all, I will never forget who this victory truly belongs to. It belongs to you. This is your victory."

3. **Use copious research sparingly:** On the surface, this sounds like a total oxymoron, but that couldn't be farther from the truth. Like the martial arts expert who never fights but rather has the quite confidence to avoid the fight, the presenter should have acquired the knowledge and discipline to be the expert on a subject, without pouring it on too heavily; nothing slows down a presentation more than too much data. And, never ever fail to attribute sources.

4. **"With" versus "to":**
Always try to engage *with* rather than present *to*. Always collaborate *with* rather than dictate *to*.

5. **Treat each slide like it's the first slide:** To the furthest extent possible, create each slide like it was the first slide of the presentation and imagine that with each slide, someone new was entering the room and needed to be caught up. This will also help your audience remember the points that you made earlier.

6. **Always employ numbers to make lists memorable:** This means to use numbers in titles of lists when you need the audience to remember them. Some examples:

   a. "The Seven Deadly Sins."

   b. "The Magnificent Seven."

   c. "The Ten Commandments."

   d. "The Five People You Will Meet in Heaven."

   e. The reason is that your brain processes numbers in dual ways. 7 and seven; 10 and ten – it creates two neural pathways. Numbers are extremely powerful and useful mnemonic devices.

7. **Use comparisons and contrasts to create strong visual images:** Information always stands out better when it is presented in contrast to something else.

   a. "You would need to eat 10 boxes of the leading brand of cereal to get as much iron as in one bowl of Total."

   b. "A million dollars is a stack of 100 dollar bills 30 inches high. A billion dollars is a stack 30 *feet* tall."

Comparisons cause the audience to draw mental pictures, and mental pictures are extremely effective ways to increase and improve memory.

8. **Use anecdotes:** People *may* remember data, they *will* remember stories. Keep them brief and to the point, but do not hesitate to use them. After displaying your expertise through the tactical employment of impressive and appropriate research, a brief anecdote

gives the audience's analytical brains a welcome rest. And once again, telling a story forces an audience to create mental pictures as it follows along, thus improving its retention of the information.

9. **Use parallel phrases:** Parallel phrase are good ways to ensure a particular point is remembered. E.g. "Viewers don't want advertising that speaks *to* them, they want advertising that speaks *with* them."

10. **Use Contrasting phrases:** "There's nothing *wrong* with America that can be fixed by what's *right* with America." – Bill Clinton.

11. **Ask questions**: One of the best ways to keep your audience engaged is to periodically pause and ask them a question. It can be as simple as pausing to ask if your audience understands everything that you have presented thus far.

12. **Do not be afraid to mention problems:** There is always a temptation to avoid bringing up problems during a presentation. People are often afraid to mention the negative, but that's a mistake. Problems are what draw an audience in and pique their interest – but, ultimately, solutions are what make them nod their heads in approval.

13. **Spread the Wealth/Share the Credit:** Always mention and thank others who have helped or provided data, or contributed in any way. You will look infinitely more confident and credible to your audience if you are willing to give credit where it is due.

14. **Avoid:** Avoid alliteration; cut the clichés; mask the metaphors; sack the similies; and, ixnay the imagery.

Get it yet?

CHAPTER FOUR: Content Part Two

People are stupid, so make it idiot-proof.

That really sounds horrible, doesn't it? I hated writing it, and I really hate the fact that I believe it to be true, but there it is. My old mentor at Telemundo, Steve, used to say: "Just when you think you've made it idiot–proof, check it again, because they just keep building better and better idiots."

I am not writing a touchy-feely, new age self-help book. There are thousands of them out there already. I am seeking to cut to the chase, and provide sound practical advice for those who really want to improve; I seek to help those who are not afraid to be a little bit politically incorrect to make their point.

This issue is especially close to my heart because nobody – and I mean *nobody* – is a greater offender than I am.

In fact, I continue to struggle with it in all of my work. There always exists the temptation to try to impress rather than to communicate clearly – it is human nature, and usually it is not even a conscious action. That is the primary reason that I stress such diligence against it.

ACTION POINT:
When you stand before an audience, you are the expert.

You are the oracle. You have the mantel of wisdom by virtue of having the floor. You are there to communicate data to that audience in a clear, concise, and hopefully entertaining way – and specifically in that order of importance: clear, concise, entertaining.

> *"Be sincere; be brief; be seated."*
> *~Franklin D. Roosevelt, on speechmaking*

It's really wonderful to be an entertaining presenter or speaker, but it is even better to be a clear one. If you don't communicate your message in a clear and concise fashion, all the jokes and anecdotes in the world are not going to get you that job, that order, or that new contract. And, never forget that your audience doesn't know what you know. You are the expert, so it is imperative that you cut out the complicated in favor of the simple.

ACTION POINT:
Simple = Honest.

Did you ever see the Oscar-winning movie *Philadelphia*? There is a wonderful scene in which Denzel Washington tells Tom Hanks: **"explain it to me as if I was a fourth grader."**

You know what? Sadly, that is probably the best piece of advice that you can possibly give to most presenters these days. And, it is more often than not that people are simply dumber than before (every generation thinks so), but because they have less time, more pressure, more distractions, and consequently shorter attention spans – to say nothing of the "digital effect" of information overload.

It is your job as the presenter to deliver your message as clearly and concisely as possible. This means boiling it down to its essence. Frequently a good comparison or metaphor will help in the process.

"If you can't explain it simply, you don't know it well enough."

— Albert Einstein

Often, the best way to determine what is truly critical to a presentation is to first go through and simply cut out everything that is not.

I like to tell clients to remember that, when Apple first launched the iPad, everyone was in arms about all the things that it did not have, the things it did not do: *It has no camera, it has no USB ports, it can't run Flash!*

But after the first week on the market they had sold over a million of them – over a million.

Too often presenters get caught up in the idea that more is better because it bolsters their argument, their point, their intelligence, or their importance.

It is important to understand that stating something in a simple manner does not need to be a sacrifice of anything – but rather a thoughtful assessment of critical to quality items.

Even in the most deeply intertwined concepts in our multi-tasking existence, we as humans can still only consider one idea at a time, thus complexity and misunderstanding often walk hand and hand.

"Simplicity is the ultimate sophistication"

— Leonardo da Vinci

CHAPTER FIVE: Packaging Part One

Guess what? You're not funny, don't tell jokes.

The best joke in the world will fail in the hands of someone without good comic timing. And, the sad truth is that precious few people can actually tell a joke. Most folks, if asked, think they are funny. They think that they can deliver a joke. Guess what? They are wrong. Letterman and Leno have teams of the brightest and funniest writers on the planet and still half of their jokes bomb. Do you really think that you are funnier than them?

It is quite hard to tell a good joke. And nothing (and I mean nothing) will kill a presentation faster than a joke that does not go over.

Some people can read the phonebook and make it sound funny. Some people can tell mundane stories and make them hilarious – Jerry Seinfeld has made a career of it. The average person cannot. The average person is most funny when relating a story about a funny incident, where the circumstances are funny. If the incident is truly funny enough, it can usually survive a poor telling.

When presenting, you have one shot. You cannot afford to roll the dice that a joke is going to hit the target. If you are dead set on a joke, ask yourself what are you seeking to gain through the telling of it: what is the end game? If you are just trying to break the ice, or relieve tension, a simple story or anecdote will work infinitely more often than a joke.

Bad Jokes Can Be Hazardous to Your Health

Research from a 2008 study by Washington State University linguist, Nancy Bell, found that people who tell bad jokes often endure an astonishing outpouring of hostility from the listeners. "The predominant verbal reaction to failed humor in our study was oriented exclusively toward attacking the speaker," Bell said.

That's just what you need. It's unlikely that an audience will throw tomatoes at you if you tell a bad joke, but it is likely that they will view you slightly differently than they did only moments ago. You enter the room the expert. You have credibility from the start. A bad joke can only serve to knock you off the pedestal that you were on when you first began your presentation.

EXERCISE: Go to your local library and look up the presentation skills books. In that section, you will find dozens of books of jokes and humor for you to use to spice up your presentations. Take a book home and read a dozen of the jokes out loud at random – and record them. Then, put the book away and go have dinner. After dinner, come back and play the recording. Do you know what you'll learn? "Yikes! I'm not funny!"

A few years back, I was working for a large broadcasting network and we had a department head who was a truly lovely person and a frightfully bad presenter. Sadly, she did not think of herself as a poor presenter and worst of all, she thought that she was quite funny.

Our company was sold, and was sold about a half dozen times during my tenure, and one of the invading hoards that took over happened to have the reputation of being a "boys club." While making her first big presentation to the "club," this department head cracked a joke about there being too many numbers in her presentation. It went something like this (I am paraphrasing):

"I know you guys have probably seen too many numbers today, and not the kind you like - the two-legged ones!"

It's really too bad that this took place in the "pre-smartphone era" because a video of the looks on the faces of the dozen or so executives sitting around the table would have been priceless. The rest of her presentation was superb. Brief slides, punctuated by short take-away thoughts for each. It was short, sweet, and in the end, utterly irrelevant. After the neutron bomb of a joke exploded, nobody was listening. They were glancing around at one another, some snickering, others rolling their eyes. Her credibility was irreparably damaged by one single, stupid joke.

I observed another 'killer' example of a joke gone array a few years ago during a major Spanish-language TV network's Upfront presentation. I am withholding the names to protect the innocent.

The presentation was to be delivered by the President of the network and the CEO, trading back and forth, each handling a section. The CEO wanted to involve one of his star talents, who would be sitting in the audience. He would clue her in beforehand so that she would be expecting the joke when it happened.

The gag was supposed to run as follows: the President of the network (who, after many many years at the company, famously still does not speak a syllable of Spanish) was going to say a few words to the audience in Spanish. Then, he was going to wink and say to them: "I've been taking lessons." Meanwhile, while he was speaking, the CEO would go out into the audience and stand next to his talent.

After the President was done, the CEO was *supposed* to say: "Wow! I'm really impressed! You've been practicing!" Then, he would turn to the talent (who spoke virtually no English) and say: "Ladies and gentleman, the star of the XXX show Ms. X! So X, what do you think of our President's

Spanish?" She was supposed to say "very good!" then give him two big thumbs up. Then, the CEO was to say: "So tell me, X, where did you learn to speak English so well?" And she was to deliver the punchline: "At the same place he learned to speak Spanish!"

I thought that the idea was horrendous. It was not even remotely funny, and even if it did not bomb, it left the door open for a potentially really weird and awkward moment.

But my pleas didn't deter our industrious CEO. The gag began as planned with the President saying his bit in Spanish, but when the spotlight turned on the CEO things began to go sideways. He had not reached the appointed spot in time and the spotlight lit the star, who turned around in complete confusion, wondering why there was a light on her. After about five seconds of bizarre awkward silence, the CEO arrived and started rambling: "So, what do you think of our President? He's been taking lessons!" Ms. X was a pro, so she smiled and laughed, but when the CEO put the mic in front of her she stammered and said: "I... ah. I... ah." And, then the CEO cut her off by saying: "Where did you learn to speak English?" He laughed and began walking back to the stage, and only then had the presence of mind to tell the audience who it was that he was talking to. But the star clearly felt that he had insulted her English skills and she stormed out of the auditorium. There were 960 people in the theater – not one laugh.

"Strange," "weird," "bizarre," and "surreal" were the words being tossed about at the after party. Another million dollar evening flushed down the toilet by an ill-conceived attempt at humor.

ACTION POINT:

If you are absolutely, totally, positively certain that your joke is going to kill - still do not do it.

Because, even if you've done it before and it has hit the mark, every audience is different and this one might be the one that does not have your sense of humor. And frankly, chances are they did not ask you to present because of your ability to tell jokes – right?

If you simply must have comedy, hire a comedian.

Top Ten List of Bad Ideas (Part Two)

1. **"Open with a joke."**

   a. *I had to mention it simply because it is sort of the elephant in the room.*

2. **"Close with a joke"**

   a. *Please refer to #1.*

3. **"You can make your voice deeper and more resonant by repeating 'Ding Dong Bing Bong King Kong' in the lowest voice possible; this helps to stretch your vocal chords."**

   a. *Google it - this tip is actually on hundreds of websites. You really cannot extend the low end of your range, due to genetics. Your vocal cords are only so long, and your throat only so large. You can, however, hurt your vocal chords – badly – if you try stupid exercises without the oversight of properly trained vocal coaches.*

4. **"Develop a ritual before each presentation and stick to it! It will increase your confidence and help you relax."**

   a. *What if something happens that cuts short your ritual? Or prevents it altogether? It is a crutch; throw it away.*

5. **"Doctors say that people of both sexes respond better to deep male voices and high female voices. Through practice, you can lower the tone of your voice."**

   a. *If you notice the tone or quality of the speaker's voice for more than the first minute, there is a problem. If you are carried away by the lush sound – red flag: distraction alert. After a minute, only the content of the material should be resonating.*

6. **"When a speaker is too polished, it makes them inaccessible to the audience."**

   a. *When was the last time you saw or heard a speaker who was too polished? Never. And, the more "polished" you become, the less "polished" you appear. You simply appear confident and natural.*

7. **"Speak to your audience at <u>Alpha</u> (8-13cps) frequencies. These are the frequencies the brain associates with pleasure and tranquility."**

   a. *Really? Time your delivery down to the frequency? New age nonsense. Another crutch; throw it away.*

8. **"Make sure to use a variety of colors and shades to your voice to keep it consistently interesting."**

   a. *Don't concern yourself with decoration, stick to the material and communicating it clearly.*

9. **"The best executives make the best presenters."**

   a. *This is true sometimes, but far less often than you would suspect.*

10. **"Always maintain a nice steady rhythm to your presentation."**

    a. *Nothing gets monotonous faster than a steady rhythm.*

    b. *Always vary your pacing, and include pauses for effect and pauses for information to sink in.*

Chapter Six: Packaging, Part Two

It's your body, learn to love it (the miracle of the smart phone).

Does anyone still use the word 'deportment'? I know that it sounds stuffy and old-fashioned, but attention to your deportment is critical, and the results are easy to see. A presenter who appears clumsy or awkward in movement, or possessing distracting physical behavior, is placing additional unecessary hurdles in the way of a successful presentation.

To some, this may seem like useless affectation, but the goal is to achieve energy without effort. On the surface, grace and elegance may appear to have little connection with the art of successful communication, but it could not be more important. Taking the stage, or entering a room with proper posture and poise, with movements that possess effortless grace, immediately suggests that a presenter is in complete command.

Effortless grace does not occur without a great deal of practice and repetition. Some presenters are blessed with it, but for the most part, it is an acquired quality. Luckily, through exercise and repitition, these skills will soon settle into your unconscious habits. And, with a body at ease, the mind will always function at a higher level and thoughts will flow more effortlessly.

That sounds great, but how do I do it?

I am still stupefied when I hear from a C-level executive that he or she does not watch video of themselves presenting.

"I hate the way that I look on camera" is the most often heard response. Guess what? If you hate the way you look, so will everybody else! It is fine: *that* is who you are. Your body is the primary medium of exchange in any presentation. The content and the language are absolutely critical, but still they are secondary and play a supporting role in the entire package.

Case One

I once had a CEO of a major cable TV network who insisted that he should present his network's programming presentation at his Upfront, rather than allow his head of programming and content to do it. He was a brilliant man and a superb broadcast executive, but he was a lousy presenter. *But he steadfastly refused to accept it.*

While rehearsing with him, I took out my phone and recorded him for about 3 minutes. Then, I played back the video on a large eight by ten presentation screen. He was *agast* at how awful he looked. He noticed his bad posture, his almost sinister habit of tapping the tips of his fingers together when he spoke, and ultimately, that he tended to look down at the floor as he paced the stage; this gave the viewing audience a prime time view of the bald spot on top of his head, but not much more.

He was furious at me for taping him without his knowledge (talk about shooting the messenger). I explained to him that it was like an "intervention." I had a contract to produce the best Upfront for them that I could, and he was the primary stumbling block preventing me from doing so. I told him that he was a good-looking man with bright eyes and a charming smile, but on stage he looked like Mr. Smithers from "The Simpsons." He looked like he was calculating a plot to take over the world, rather than sharing the good news about his upcoming slate of new fall shows.

He reluctantly agreed to work with me on "only the physicality of the presentation, the blocking and movement." It was not what I wanted, but it was all I was going to get from him, and something was better than nothing.

It was almost too easy. After two hours of working with him, we re-read the exact same portion of the presentation and I videoed him again. Watching the playback, he was nodding his head and smiling. The difference was really night and day.

(**Author's note:** The CEO never re-hired me. But the check did clear...oh well.)

Case Two

Another great example that I was present for was that of a television network sales representative who was being asked to present at a national sales conference for the first time.

She was a very attractive woman, tall with long dark hair. She was very pleasant and charming when you spoke to her one-on-one, but whenever she got up in front of people – even in a small boardroom – she became a different person. The charm disappeared, replaced by a tough, all-business demeanor that bordered on anger.

Her presentation content was fine; in fact, it was quite good, but there was something missing from the overall picture. She seemed cold and detached from the material. I could not put my finger on exactly what the problem was until we recorded her doing the same presentation.

At first, I thought that it was just a case of simple nerves, but that wasn't it; she was cool as a cucumber. She did not have any of the typical distracting behaviors (too much hand movement, touching of the hair, etc.), but something kept her at arms-length from the audience.

Then it dawned on me. I asked her if she noticed it, too, and she said something interesting: "I look angry." She was right. Prior to getting up in front of her team, she was all smiles and laughter, but once in the spotlight, she did not smile, not even once, for nearly seven minutes. She was not engaged with her material or her audience. She stated that she was always afraid that, if she looked like she was having fun, no one would take her seriously. This was an interesting observation. I assured her that being serious and being angry were worlds apart.

Not to get overly political, but at a time when our country still refuses to guarantee women in the workplace equal wages for equal work, it is reasonable for a female employee to feel that she needs to work harder, do better, be smarter, etc., than her counterparts to get equal respect for her work.

I asked her if she ever heard the expression: "if you are having a good time on stage, then your audience will have a good time. If you look tense, then your audience will be tense." At the end of the day, she was putting a great deal of energy into a defensive posture that was not helping her with her delivery. We recorded her several more times, and little by little, she began to enjoy herself delivering the presentation.

Finally, I told her that I wanted her to do the presentation one more time, but this time with the biggest fake smile plastered on her face for the entire duration of the presentation. I wanted to see nothing but teeth from start to finish.

She only got through about 30 seconds before she nearly fell over laughing. Once she regained her composure, I told her: "ok, one big cleansing breath and take it from the top – any way you feel comfortable."

It was like night and day. She was delightful. She opened her presentation with a warm, welcoming smile. She proceeded to move through her data in a thoughtful manner, even tossing in a funny unplanned anecdote that hit the bulls-eye. Finally, she closed with a big smile and asked if there were any questions.

I immediately pulled out the disc of her first presentation, and we sat and watched the two back to back. She cringed as she watched the first tape (although it really was not that bad at all) and said: "I can't believe that for ten years, that was my public persona." I quickly corrected her, because it was not her public persona but her presenting persona (if you will). She was always the superb sales person that she knew herself to be, but now she had the confidence to elevate her game to the next level.

Case Three

The last anecdote that I will share on this subject pertains to the CEO of a major international corporation. He was an extraordinarily intelligent man, who spoke no less than six languages fluently. He had lived in countries on six continents, and had run major companies in each.

He was a superb speaker. He had a magnificently booming, gravelly baritone voice reminiscent of Gregory Peck. I loved to hear him speak, but I hated to *watch* him speak. He suffered from the worst case of "happy hands" of anyone I had ever encountered. One moment, he was gesturing like the Pope, and the next, he was the Queen of England; next, he was an Italian waiter extoling the glories of tonight's *Osso Bucco* special.

He was by far my most difficult case, specifically because he was so successful. Along with that success came the absolute unshakeable conviction that he knew everything better than everybody else.

I was producing an event designed to introduce his new company to the New York advertising community, and he was the keynote speaker for the evening. I had seen him speak only once before, and I immediately got nervous. All I could think was: "How the hell did this guy get so far, with these presentation skills?" It became clear very quickly that he had surrounded himself with a hoard of yes-men and women, all of whom thought he walked on water. Obviously, none of them would ever drop even a hint of constructive criticism. Well, they were doing him no favors.

A few weeks before the event, I asked him if we could do a dry-run of his speech in his board room – for running time purposes. He readily agreed. I set up my phone on the big round table of the board room and recorded his presentation. When he was complete, he smiled and asked: "So? What do you think? Too long? Too short?"

I told him that I thought the length was just fine, in fact better than fine, just right for this event. Then, I crossed the bridge and said: "Would you like to watch playback?"

He said: "Sure." Then, I did something sneaky: I played the video back at 1 ½ speed and turned the sound off. I told him: "I would like to share a really tiny observation I made, that you might want to give some thought, too."

He watched the video for about a minute, and called out: "I look like a Goddamn monkey! Turn this off. Why are you showing this to me?"

He was really angry. I said to him that the increased speed was just to make a point. "You really do tend to gesture with your hands quite a bit when you speak. Are you aware of that?"

He said that it was for emphasis and dramatic effect, and to keep his audience's attention. I told him that I thought he was a fantastic communicator without the gestures and that a more measured use of them might seem more authoritative and commanding. We ran the speech again and he tried to limit his movements; it was a total disaster. I was sure that he was going to fire me. As his frustration grew, I told him to stop trying to calculate when is best to use a gesture; it makes you uncomfortable. "Here is a suggestion: try putting one hand behind your back, right around the small of your back, and keep it there. Let the other hand run wild."

He started again, and after a rocky 10-20 seconds, he was spectacular. I quickly turned on the camera to grab the moment. He strode around looking supremely confident, while at the same time, thoughtful and passionate. Once freed form the tether of his other hand, his free hand became a source of power and authority. And best yet, his beautiful speaking voice shined through even more clearly with fewer distractions.

I immediately replayed the video, and he was positively giddy. After it was over, he turned to me and said: "You really must write a book! You have improved my communication immeasurably in five minutes" (the genesis of the title of the book).

ACTION POINT:

Don't hide your emotions; use them. They are real and genuine. They make a presenter more authentic and honest to an audience.

The CEO and the Sales person that we discussed are not alone. In fact, most people have a radically different self-image than the one the public actually sees. Most of us have never even seen what we look like in a moving picture. Of course, we know what we look like in still photographs, but on video we are often startled at what we see. The camera is unforgiving. It shows you warts and all, it shows you as your public actually sees you. It can be hard to watch sometimes, but it is the easiest and most effective way of improving your presentation skills quickly and dramatically.

Begin by watching the presentation in its entirety, without taking any notes. You are simply looking for an overall impression. When you are done, write down your broad-stroke observations. Did you like it? Was it too long?

Then watch it again, this time with either your outline or your ORSON chart in front of you. This time take copious notes and annotate them on the chart where they occur.

Pay attention to your:

- Overall deportment

- Demeanor

- Posture

- Distracting movements

- Use of hand gestures

- Distracting facial expressions

As you do, don't think about how to fix them (yet). Place yourself in the audience and think about how those particular items made you feel and *write that down*. Ask yourself if these are the feelings that you wanted to elicit from your presentation.

ACTION POINT:
We are blessed with technology – use it!

As recently as even ten years ago, the process of recording yourself was a big hassle. Nowadays, everybody on the planet has a video camera on their phone. You absolutely must tape yourself presenting. Do it over again. I promise you that, each and every time you do, you will find something else you can improve.

Those feelings that you jotted down to best describe your overall impressions; take them out now. One by one, look at them, and then write down what the ideal response would have been. Then, outline brief steps that could bridge the gap between the observed and the desired effect.

Once you are done tweaking, you will be happy with what you see, and your confidence will go through the roof. And, when confidence rises, everything about the presentation improves as well.

Voice

Once you are happy with yourself visually, and you feel confident, you are ready to take it to the next level. Fade out the video or turn away from the screen and focus exclusively on your voice and your verbal delivery.

For the first time that you listen, close your eyes and visualize yourself in the audience listening to this speaker. Don't take any notes at all, just listen. When you are done, write down your immediate impressions.

Next, print out a copy of your outline or your ORSON chart and have it in front of you while you listen. This time, take copious notes. Listen to every syllable and every vocal inflection and decide what you like and what you do not. Once again, that is what the public is hearing. That is your public voice. Is it higher than you thought? Probably. Our ear canals tend to amplify the lower range of tones in our own voice. You need to embrace the person on the video and accept that it is him or her that is stating your case for you!

We will talk more about specifics of the voice in detail later; here, all we want to achieve is a level of comfort with yourself.

Being comfortable in front of people is a gift from God. But, just because you are comfortable before an audience, it doesn't mean that you are a good presenter. I have met and worked with numerous speakers who were so in love with themselves that they had no problem whatsoever getting up in front of a thousand people. Many were very good presenters as well; just as many were awful.

ACTION POINT:
They are here for the material, not for you.

There's nothing more boring than listening to a presenter who is clearly in love with himself. There is nothing more interesting that listening to a presenter who is clearly in love with his material.

Know your body.

Video is, again, the fastest and easiest way to acquaint yourself with your body as the world sees it. I mentioned the issue of posture before, but it is critical to hammer it home. As we get older, our old friend gravity tends to pull us closer to the earth. And, in doing so, causes us to slouch forward, to keep out hand and arms in front of us rather than at our sides, and it causes our heads to jut forward in front of our shoulders.

Chiropractors tell us that the proper alignment for our bodies is for our ears to be directly above our shoulders. Are yours? Mine certainly are not. But, if you watch a ballet dancer walk across a stage, you will see strength, poise, and confidence. Every presenter in the world could learn a lesson from them. Of course, their gracefulness is the result of thousands of hours of hard work acquiring the discipline. Presumably, you do not have that much time, but you do have eyes and you can emulate.

Ballet Dancer as Presenter

Remember when I told you that I wasn't going to bother you about your posture? I lied. By now, I think that you can take it.

Begin by imagining you have long hair. Now imagine that it is tied in a long braid from the top back of your head. Now, imagine someone is pulling straight up on the braid. Your head will naturally move backwards and up. It is a very simple exercise that you should try, and do it in front of a mirror to see the difference it makes in your entire body language. You will find that your chest will come slightly forward, your shoulders slightly back. You will immediately display a significantly more "open" stance.

ACTION POINT:

Psychologists tell us that, on an intrinsic level, open means honest.

CHAPTER SEVEN: Packaging Part Three

I don't glow, I sweat...a lot. How to deal with flop sweats.

"You may not realize it, but a major portion of speech anxiety actually comes from nervousness."

This brilliant tidbit is an actual quote from a major speech coach in a book co-written by an Ivy League University, and published by a major book publisher. It is precisely the kind of useless nonsense that we have been warning you against in this book thus far.

I will not waste readers' time with any such new age nonsense. We will stick to simple practical techniques that you can employ immediately.

"The best way to conquer stage fright is to know what you're talking about."

- Michael H. Mescon

A wonderful acting teacher that I know in New York once told me it is all about giving yourself permission. I have observed her teach often and was struck by the reaction that she gets when she tells her students: "when you stand before an audience, you need to give yourself permission to be up there, to deserve to be the authority." In essence, your brain needs to *allow* you to be the expert, to free yourself from doubt. You have every right to be there. Your thoughts and insights are valuable. You can state your case with confidence.

Breathe. Move. Swallow. Repeat.

Your body goes into fight or flight mode when you are frightened. That is the most basic Darwinian concept. When Cro-Magnon man sensed danger, his brain sent a message to his adrenal gland to create more adrenalin. More adrenalin increased his heart rate and forced blood to all the extremities. He was in a fight for his life, or a flight for his life, and he needed the extra energy and increased circulation. Those who did not often wound up dinner for someone.

Nowadays, we have many fewer and fewer man-eating animals, and hardly any are socialized enough to be in the conference room where you are about to speak.

Nonetheless, that primordial urge of fight or flight remains. That urge that kept your ancestors out of the mouths of lions and sabre toothed tigers now makes your hands cold as ice and your heart race before speaking in public.

The best way that I have found for dealing with this is a Zen Buddist-based technique of breathing. It goes right to the heart of the problem and gives you great control over your body. It requires time and work to perfect, but it almost always works. However, to be an efficient practitioner, you need to invest many months of practice.

ACTION POINT:
Your breath is your fuel.

It is the medium and driving force of your voice. There are actually thousands of deep breathing exercises, so I will not belabor the point, but five to six minutes of even the most basic breathing application before speaking is a good idea. For our purposes, I am going to address the symptoms and not the cause, simply because you do not have time. In fact, you never have time. Nobody has time to acquire any real discipline nowadays, myself included.

So, here are a few life-saving techniques that I have employed to great success on numerous occasions.

Technique One

Ice water: This one runs counter intuitive to all advice to keep the body warm and free of tension. I only recommend it in extreme cases.

It takes the average human heart one minutes to complete a Venus cycle. By that, I mean the amount of time that it takes for your blood to complete an entire tour of your body and return to the heart.

Ten minutes before you are due to speak, or before an interview, head for the rest room and turn on the cold water. Let the water run for a minute or two to get cold. Then, roll up your shirt sleeves and place your wrists under the cold water. Keep them there for five minutes, or until you begin to get a brain freeze.

Did he just say "brain freeze"?

Yes. Running the cold water over your wrists for an extended period of time will cool the blood as it circulates. Eventually, it will cool your entire core. It will also cool all the veins and capillaries on the top of your head and under your arms that cause you to sweat. This does not address the bigger problem, but it typically provides a quick and effective means to cool down before going into the lion's den.

Technique Two

Movement: A few years ago, the magnificent Tony-winning actor, dancer, and clown, Bill Irwin was performing at a benefit for a local arts center. He was going to tell a few stories and do a dance performance art piece with a young man playing the cello. It was a scream. The audience howled. Bill tore the house down.

So why am I mentioning him in a chapter about flop sweats?

Before he went on, he stood alone backstage for about 20 minutes. In that time, he stretched out like a world class athlete. In addition, he did something that I had never seen before: he shook every single muscle group in his body. He did not simply shake them, he looked like he was having an epileptic fit. He worked his lower extremities, then his torso. Then, he shook his arms like a rag doll. Finally, he shook his head, neck, and jaws. When he was done, he did what appeared to be a few long, lean yoga stretches, followed by several deep cleansing breaths.

Any tightness, stress, or muscle tension was long gone. Here was clearly a master at work. For the record, I do not recommend flailing like a rag doll in public. However, in the quiet of a rest room, I do – whole heartedly. Releasing the stress from your muscles is the best favor that you can possibly do for yourself before a presentation. It is the simplest and most effective way of relaxing I know of.

Technique Three

HYDRATE. Recently, a Republican Senator was delivering the Republican rebuttal to the President's State of the Union address. Halfway through, the Senator was so cotton-mouthed that he had to awkwardly lunge off camera to grab a bottle of water. Then, he took a deep long swig of it – *on camera.* It was the behavior of a rank amateur and not that of a U.S. Senator. How is it possible that, before the biggest presentation of his career and a world-wide audience, he was so completely unprepared? He sounds like the type of person who needs to keep to-do lists.

Sadly, he's not alone.

The CEO of a major TV network that I worked at was delivering his upfront presentation at the Museum of Natural History in New York. In front of a packed house, right in the middle of his presentation, he rather ostentatiously produced a large bottle of water. It almost looked like a product placement for the company Poland Springs. The spotlight reflected off of it beautifully as the CEO strode across the stage. He even got so comfortable holding it that he used it to punctuate his statements – then he would take deep swigs from it while his videos played.

Of course, at the after party, the water bottle was all anyone remembered about the presentation. It was a running joke for months afterwards:

"This Network Upfront was brought to you by Poland Spring!"

"Poland Spring, the choice of parched presenters everywhere."

Here is a company that was rumored to have spent upwards of a million dollars on its Upfront presentation, and all anyone took away from the evening was a handful of bad jokes about the CEO and a water bottle. It had completely undermined the message - money well-spent.

What do we learn from this? Always drink a copious amount of water 5-10 minutes before you speak, but no longer that 10 minutes before. The idea is not to have to go to the rest room during the presentation. It is ideal to have several short sips before going on just to moisten your mucus membranes. Also, remember to try and drink room temperature water; cold water can vaso-constrict your vocal chords, to a degree, and in some cases, create unwanted tension. However, if you already feel your body beginning to overheat, cold water can be your best friend and the likelihood that it will tense your cords is minimal.

Keep a tall glass of water just out of sight either in a podium or on a table closeby (closer than the Republican Senator did). A glass always looks more elegant than a plastic water bottle.

If you are on a job interview, always ask for water when you enter, even if you don't need it. Knowing that you have it in case of emergency can relieve stress on a sub-conscious level.

Technique Four

Tic-Tacs. Placing one Tic-Tack in the back of your mouth between your cheek and gums, or under your tongue and against your gums, just before you speak will typically cause you to salivate more than enough to keep you from getting dry-mouth during your presentation.

What if I should get the flop swears during my presentation?

This is definitely not good. The second that you begin to feel yourself sweating, you get more nervous, which causes you to sweat more, which makes you more nervous, which causes you to sweat more, which makes you more nervous – and so on.

Generally, flop sweats are a temporary condition lasting just a few minutes, and always at the very beginning of a presentation or an interview. Sometimes, just knowing that they are going to stop is enough to calm you. But, the best way that I know to block the sweats once you feel them begin, is to completely block them out. Do not exert one single thought about it.

Easier said than done, but not impossible. The following technique is the best way that I know of.

Technique Five

Material, material, material. Concentrate completely on the material that you are presenting – *only* on the material. *Dive* into the material. You must cease to exist and leave only the material. Like an actor who loses his or herself in a part, lose yourself in the material. Do not give even a hint of thought to the perspiration. Don't just ignore it, don't notice it at all! There is only the presentation, the material. Forget for a moment that there is even an audience.

> *If need be, for a moment, turn away from the audience and point to a fact or figure in the presentation. Draw their attention away from you, and toward the screen or computer.*

As the audience's attention leaves you and attends to the point that you are making, you will immediately feel a visceral difference. The energy of their focus being diverted will give you the time to allow your body to recompose itself. The body is the most magnificent instrument in the universe, and it can be played like a Stradivarius. You merely need to practice – a lot.

Wow, I don't know the answer to that.

Everyone is asked a question now and again that they do not know the answer to. It is not a crime or a sin. Understand, nobody can be an expert on absolutely every aspect of everything. Stating in a calm and honest manner that you do not have the answer will almost always leave the audience or interviewer with a generally positive impression.

ACTION POINT:

You do not want to start making apologies or excuses. This will only belabor the point and possibly compromise your integrity in their eyes.

Above all, do not lie, become defensive, or evasive. If you do, you will fail. You will get apprehensive and distracted. Frequently, your ability to remain calm when you do not know the answer will be regarded much more highly than a bad answer.

I used to work at a major television network; I was there for many years. About a decade ago, a new CEO was brought on board. At his first national sales conference, he was asked a question that (in retrospect) he did not have the answer to, but his answer was so artful and well-constructed that the audience felt that he had answered perfectly well.

I will paraphrase his remark:

"I'm glad you asked that question, because it is something that has been on my mind quite a bit lately, and frankly, I am still of two minds on it. There are a lot of conflicting opinions about exactly what the right approach is, and at this point, we are really still drilling down through the data. I promise you that we are going to have an answer for you very soon, but I think to give one today would be just a little bit premature."

Now that's an answer; every word perfectly chosen and articulated with surgical precision. Did any of you happened to catch what exactly he actually said? Correct – he said nothing. However, he said it well. So, what is the bottom line?

ACTION POINT:

Always emphasize what you *do* know and follow with *how you will find out* what you do not know.

If you know yourself to be less artful than our aforementioned CEO, here are a couple of ideas how to deal with questions that you do not know the answer to:

Follow Up

"I really should know that, but I do not have the answer right off the top of my head. Please give me your e-mail address after the presentation, and I will get right back to you."

A Higher Authority

"I have an opinion on that, but I know someone who can answer it better. I will get his name for you."

Audience Petition

"That is a great question. Did everybody hear it? I have an opinion on it, but I am more curious to hear what some of you think about this."

Once again, what is most critical is the grace with which you handle the question.

CHAPTER EIGHT: **Passion Part One**

Elements of Style *(apologies to Strunk and White)*

- *Stand.*
- *Move away from the podium.*
- *Out from behind the presenter table.*
- *Keep your hands out of your pockets.*
- *Don't tilt your head.*
- *Stand up straight.*
- *Don't pace too much.*
- *Walk more.*
- *Make eye contact with more people.*
- *Make eye contact with fewer people.*
- *Gesture bigger.*
- *Gesture smaller.*

Are you tired of this crap? I know that I am.

All of these suggestions appear in countless books on improving your speaking or presentation skills. Every single one of them *might* work for you, but most will not. Why do you think that is? Nothing replaces work, end of story. The amount of improvement that you will see will be a direct proportion of the amount of work that you put into it.

ACTION POINT:
Skill = Talent X Work

Delivery: Eliminating "Crutches and Distractions"

Noted acting teacher Jay Goldenberger has a wonderfully concise expression that he uses with his students:

"Too much decoration!"

He is absolutely correct. Nothing makes a presentation look more thread bare than "too much decoration." He stresses to his students the importance of being "in the moment," "immediacy," and eliminating the window dressing.

In this section, dedicated to your delivery, we will cover a few physical aspects, and stress eliminating "crutches" and "distractions" (the decorations); these things get in the way of clear, honest, and authentic presentation.

The truth is that there are millions of tiny aspects of every single presentation and that they are really difficult to put into nice little groups. There are physical, emotional, mental, and environmental issues to deal with each time you get up to speak. You would need volumes to deal with every aspect. But, rather than try to categorize every aspect, we will deal with some of the more critical, broad-strokes issues.

Training your body physically is a process, but it is a process that will, in the end, result in greater creative freedom, as you develop more flexibility and sensitivity in your presenting.

Weight Training for Speakers

Well, in a manner of speaking. Recently, I worked with another CEO who also suffered from "happy hands" that I had ever encountered. He was a fine presenter in most respects, but he had the annoying habit of gesturing with his hands to accentuate every sentence that he uttered. A good portion of the gestures were completely extraneous and needed to be curbed.

I employed my trusted Sony Flip Camcorder and shot him delivering a brief presentation to his sales force. As in the previous cases, we watched the playback with the sound off and took notes. I did not need to say a word; he immediately saw that his hands were out of control.

He was an open-minded executive and not averse to trying something slightly unorthodox. I brought two small 5 pound hand weights to the office and gave them to him. At first, he looked at me with a surprised look, but he played along. I then asked him to do the exact same presentation that he'd done the day before, but this time, I wanted him to hold the weights in his hand.

The initial results were not encouraging at all. He was almost incapable of speaking without using his hands. He was enormously frustrated at first, but it made him more resolute. Before long, he became more comfortable with less hand movement, and keeping his hands by his side (a place that they rarely visited before).

Despite the impediment of the weights, certain points in his speech were important enough to him that he still gestured with his hands. He told me that he made mental notes when they occurred, because he realized that they had organically risen to the top of his priority list.

We then watched the play back. Excepting the first few moments where he looked very uncomfortable and awkward, the presentation was infinitely more impressive. Important issues were given appropriate weight (no pun intended), and the gestures punctuated the presentation. Additionally, insignificant points did not distract from the critical focus of the presentation.

The Grammar of the Hands

People inherently get bored by static objects, so it is important to maintain a certain amount of movement and energy to propel the presentation forward. It is also true that audiences tend to remember messages better if they reach multiple senses. But it is equally important for the body language and the information conveyed to be complementary of one another. In other words, do not let it become a distraction.

ACTION POINT:

Rule of thumb: the less gestures the better.

Exercise

Try doing your entire presentation standing still with your hands at your sides. Spoiler alert: it is much harder than you think. I promise you that although it will be uncomfortable and unnatural at first, you will almost forget about them after a while. Much like the CEO with the dumbbells, you should slowly begin to reintegrate your hands into the presentation, using them primarily as "punctuation" of ideas.

Once again, you need to decide for yourself just how much you think is appropriate – and video remains the best way to make a cold, sober assessment.

Quality of the Voice

Never try to be something you are not. If you are not blessed with the voice of James Earl Jones, or Morgan Freeman, that is fine. Do not ever try to speak in a voice that is not entirely your own. It is another distraction that only distances you from your material and your audience.

When Frank Sinatra asked Luciano Pavarotti: "How can I get the kind of volume and power you get when you sing?" Pavarotti told him: "First, you need to open your mouth when you sing."

If time and money were no object, I would recommend that every single person who has to give more than one presentation per year take voice lessons. A traditional singing teacher will provide all the elements that make a strong, healthy, and powerful speaking voice. My ex-wife was an opera singer, and from sitting through hundreds of hours of her lessons, I learned more about how to breathe, proper breath control, articulation, pronunciation, and enunciation than I learned in all of the books on presentation skills combined.

These teachers are the real deal because there is no hiding it in opera. But understanding the governing principles means nothing without being able to apply them in a real life situation - you need to get up and speak, often.

You cannot change the voice that you have been given, but you can control its pitch, pace, volume, and inflection.

ACTION POINT:
Write it down - always take notes.

When listening to the playback of the audio of your presentation, have a copy of your ORSON sheet in front of you. Once again, as you listen, take notes on each section as it relates to pitch, pace, volume, and inflection. Listen to see if your voice inflects upwards during the questions, and downward at the completion of a thought. Check to see if you are speaking at the exact speed and rhythm that you want to be while making your most critical points.   You will find you can improve the overall impact of your speech or presentation significantly in no time at all by making the smallest of corrections.

ACTION POINT:
Just because something is small does not mean it is insignificant.

The Power of the Pause

> *"The most precious things in speech are the pauses."*
>
> *- Sir Ralph Richardson*

A few years ago, while watching the Vice President of Sales at NBC give a presentation at a conference, I noticed the *single most important lesson* anyone could ever learn about presentation giving. I would be *definitely remiss* if I neglected to share it with you. If you remember *nothing else at all in this entire book*, remember this:

(insert sound effect of Crickets Chirping)

At this point, whatever I said, no matter how mundane or immaterial would be branded into your memory bank.

It is remarkable, and it works absolutely every single time. Have you ever seen the comedian Bill Engval?   He has a comedy routine based around giving people signs that say "I'm stupid" on them.   His punch line is simple and hilarious: "Here's your sign!" That is sort of what the Vice President of Sales was doing – with a lot more panache and subtlety.

First comes the big build up, then the bigger build up, then the biggest build up, followed by the pregnant pause for dramatic effect is a *fool-proof* way to make certain that your most important piece of data is always remembered.

Whenever I am coaching a speaker, and we are approaching the critical focus of the presentation, I will say: "okay, now paint them a sign!" And, they know exactly what to do. I would not recommend adding a great deal of extended pauses to any one presentation, but a carefully placed one is an extremely powerful tool. Use them judiciously.

I saw that Vice President of Sales use this particular technique over and over again in presentation after presentation, and it never missed the mark, and it never felt stale.

> *"The right word may be effective, but no word was ever as effective as a rightly timed pause."*
>
> *- Mark Twain*

CHAPTER NINE: Passion Part Two

Memory you improve to how ... *say what?*

Ever notice that newscasters rarely make mistakes when reading from the teleprompter? This is not only true for big network newscasters but even small town news. Are they all amazingly proficient readers and speakers?

Well, presumably they are. Do you believe it? Of course not. They have polished their skills through countless repetitions, and they do it every single day; they also employ very simple exercises to help their brains recognize the copy even before they read it.

As I've stated about almost every other point in this book, some presenters are blessed with a retentive memory, but most are not. In their case, a retentive memory is not a gift but a skill, a habit, and like all good habits it is acquired through continual, careful work. Memorization is nothing more than simply a systematic association of ideas and images.

ACTION POINT:
Never memorize – always *almost* memorize.

If you try to memorize or copy a speech, during your presentation, you will focus your energy in the recall of the words and not in the delivery of them.

ACTION POINT:

One hundred percent of your energy should be spent in the delivery of the words, every single time you open your mouth.

So, how do you help your brain get familiar with your material? To begin, always focus on the meaning of what you are saying, the points you are trying to get across, rather than the exact words. That way, if for some reason, you are interrupted, you will not struggle to pick up the thread of what you were saying.

Then, begin to read your material multiple times until you are capable of anticipating the upcoming words before your active brain reads them.

Once you reach that point, stop.

Then, go to the very end of your presentation or speech and read the entire speech word by word backwards. Make sure to read it aloud.

It will be extremely awkward, and even difficult, but shortly your brain will start recognizing that the words are the same ones that you just read earlier. Do this several times and you will notice your speed increase exponentially. Once this occurs, stop.

Now, go back to the top of the script and read it forwards. You will be astonished at how much easier the material flows from you. When that occurs, you will immediately feel less stress. Consequentially, you will feel more confident, and you will be able to devote more energy to the specific delivery of the words and the message that they contain. The result will always sound more extemporaneous when you possess freedom and spontaneity in your delivery; your presentation will be the direct result of well considered thought process rather than merely an endeavor to remember words.

Congratulations! Wasn't that easy?

Digital Assistance

Reading your words aloud help trigger retention but so does simply listening to them. It is helpful for a presenter to make his or her workouts, chores, driving, and recreational activities into learning sessions. Recording your ORSON points as an mp3 file, and then listening to them repeatedly with the help of your phone or your music player, will help ingrain them and create yet another neural pathway.

The Importance of Movement

Studies have shown that *active experiencing*, defined as the use of "all physical, mental, and emotional channels to communicate the meaning of material to another person," is an extremely effective way to help retain information. This principle is widely used by stage actors and is now being used increasingly in academia to help students retain information.

It can be a simple as reading your material sitting, followed by reading it while standing, and then reading it while moving about. To the furthest extent possible, you want to incorporate as many of the gestures that you will use at the actual presentation. Ultimately, the more guestures and body movements you incorporate, the more you will retain through "active experiencing."

CHAPTER TEN: **Passion Part Three**

If you love the material, so will your audience.

By now, you have likely noticed the word that I use more often than any other in the context of presenting is honesty. Have you figured out why? The answer is simple, but complex: it is simple in that it is fairly obvious; it is complex in that it has many applications and works on many levels.

The simple: you are saying, "Of course it helps to be honest." Really, why? What benefit does it provide? Think about it for a moment. I recently asked a group of college seniors this very question and none could come up with an answer. They all said they "kinda sorta" knew but could not be specific. So, what is so important about being honest when you get up to speak?

Unless you are a pathological liar (and I have met several) or a sociopath (have not met any yet), you are intrinsically less comfortable being dishonest than you are being honest. It is biology. It is human nature. And, when I speak of honesty, I am not speaking exclusively about telling lies, I am speaking on a far more subtle level: being intellectually dishonest, being emotionally dishonest, selling ideas or products we do not believe in, or do not believe are what they claim to be or to the extent that they claim to be.

And yet, we all have to do it periodically. One CEO told me, "On one level or another, we are selling with every word we speak."

A great broadcasting executive who was my mentor in many ways, Steve Levin, former Head of Sales for the Telemundo Network, put it this way: "We're not curing cancer and we're not feeding starving children. We're selling TV airtime." A little perspective goes a long way. After all, you want to build trust and credibility, to be honest and credible.

ACTION POINT:

The goal is not perfection; the goal is honesty and passion.

It's Hard to Say Goodbye

How you close your presentation is critical. It is your final chance to make absolutely certain your audience takes away the critical data you are seeking to empart. Recall what we discussed in the first chapter about the core purpose of any speech or presentation:

- Provide the audience with the proper information.
- Persuade the audience to come to the proper conclusion.

ACTION POINT:

A closing statement should be short, clear, and unambiguous.

So, in your final moments as the "oracle," the expert, how do we make certain that happens? After observing numerous presentations with the specific purpose of studying how the speaker elected to close, I observed a few trends emerging.

Quotations

Quite a few chose to end with a quote. A well-chosen quote can be extremely effective. A quotation provides additional evidence and support to your case. However, it is important to remember that, whenever integrating a quote into a presentation, you must move quickly and smoothly from the quote to its relevance to your own argument. You also need to make sure you do not use the quotations to tell the story for you. Ideally, your reason for choosing a particular quote will be immediately self-evident – but not always. It is critical to reinforce the context. An inappropriate use of a quotation can be deadly to a presentation.

Anecdotes

For millennia, mankind has learned through the experience of others. The Bible is full of anecdotes, and parables were the favored method of teaching of Jesus Christ. So, if it is good enough for Jesus…

As I have stated repeatedly throughout the book, I am a fan of anecdotes for a whole host of reasons (it is not necessary to restate them again). That being said, I do not like to use them as closings for speeches or presentations. The reason is simple: by definition, anecdotes require a connection of thoughts by the listener to the story being told, in hope of them arriving at the desired conclusion. In short, it is not direct enough.

You want to leave your audience, or your interview, with the complete conviction that you stated your case and your audience understood completely and clearly what it was you were trying to communicate. In that respect, you are not merely responsible for communicating your information, you are also responsible for making absolutely certain that your audience understood it!

For that reason, the type of closing that is generally most effective almost exclusively is one that clearly outlines the choices that need to be made, and the consequences thereof.

Drawing a Contrast

This is easily my most preferred method of closing a presentation. State your thesis in plain black and white terms, and state the consequences of action or inaction.

This method fully engages the audience because it places responsibility on them. It makes them an active participant in the outcome. It is a clear-cut call to action.

"We can choose to fix this problem, and reap the benefit of our actions - or, we can continue the course/status quo and have to live with the continued results of our inaction. The choice is yours."

Obviously, these words are meant only to be representative and exact words should be tailored case by case. The point is that it illustrates just how impactful and effective concluding with a strong rhetorical question, one that captures and crystalizes the message and the stakes, can be. It answers our initial purpose:

- Provide the audience with the proper information.
- Persuade the audience to come to the proper conclusion.

It leaves the audience with a question, a responsibility, an assignment, and that equals engagement.

"If you have an important point to make, don't try to be subtle or clever. Use a pile driver. Hit the point once. Then come back and hit it again. Then hit it a third time - a tremendous whack."

- Winston Churchill

CHAPTER ELEVEN

You can learn a lot from an actor.

I have already used anecdotes about actors and acting teachers to illustrate several points and concepts earlier in the book. The reason is simple: nobody does it better.

This chapter could be a book unto itself because, much like presenting, there is not one single right way to act.

Last year, a play that I had written was chosen for a staged reading by a regional performing arts center. I was lucky enough to secure the distinguished director Gabriel Barre to direct it. During the first read through with him, he gave me a piece of advice that I now give to all of my clients.

He said: "Before we read through the play, why don't you go thought it and remove all of the bolding, italicizing, underlining, and exclamation points." I told him that I thought that would rob the story of all its theatricality and style. With a wink, he said: "Maybe, but it might just distill it down to its essence." In a sense, free it of its bonds of "context" and allow the pure message to flow though. In addition, it freed the actors to interpret the words unfettered by my clumsy suggestions.

It was a revelation. Whenever you are preparing a presentation, (this is especially true in the case of a straight speech) remove all the bolding, highlighting, italics, and underlining. Then, read the speech back aloud and see how it sounds. Then, slowly, reintroduce those elements in a considered fashion. You will generally find that you have achieved a far more judicious use of them. Your presentation will be much more focused and cogent.

"The minute you walked in the joint…"

Appearances count. I have a friend who is one of the most popular and sought after talent agents in the Motion Picture industry. She once told me "that 80% of auditions are over before the actor even opens their mouth."

The point that she makes is universal. Every time you have an interview, speech, or presentation to give, you are being judged *not* from the minute you begin to speak, but rather from the minute you walk into the room. Everything counts because everything creates an impression, from the clothes you're wearing to the way you walk, the way you smile, and the way you shake hands.

It is important to understand, that relatively speaking, it is easy to be in control of the expressiveness of your face and of your hands – but remember that you are being judged by your entire package. Do not create an unnecessary handicap for yourself to overcome.

So, the next time that you are telling yourself, while getting ready for a presentation, that there is no need for a tie because the audience is laid back, think again.

ACTION POINT:
It is always better to be a little bit overdressed rather than underdressed.

I like to tell clients to have a plan – not a detailed or rigid one – for what you are going to do in the moments before your presentation. The reason for this is simple. Too much dead time before the presentation can cause you to start thinking about changing little things; it can cause you to think that you can get it just a little bit better, tighter, or faster.

ACTION POINT:
Never make changes in the eleventh hour.

I can say conclusively that 99 percent of the last minute changes that I have made to clients' presentations over 20 years have diminished their presentations.

One in particular comes to mind. I spent over a month writing and producing the Upfront presentation for a major television network. I worked with the CEO and the head of sales refining their presentations and coaching their on-stage movements. It was running like a Swiss watch.

Then, after the final run through (90 minutes before curtain), the CEO came to me and introduced his new Vice President of Marketing. He asked me to show her the presentation on my computer, which I did. He then showed incomprehensively bad judgment and asked her: "Is there anything you think we should change?" I politely jumped in and told him that the presentation was "locked" and no changes could be made. Unfortunately, the CEO decided that nothing was locked until he said so. I explained that all of our lighting and A/V cues were in place and could not be changed. We had a big name artist poised to hit the stage with his band immediately after the final video. It was all tightly choreographed. Still, he pressed on and again asked her for her opinion. She did not possess the fortitude to say the right thing. She reluctantly said: "Well, perhaps at the very end we could do a final slide recapping our two new shows."

Of course, the CEO loved the idea. He personally dictated two new slides to the PowerPoint operator on the fly moments before we went live. I continued to argue to no avail. He had no verbage for the last slide – nor did we know who was going to deliver the as yet unwritten verbage. He decided that he was just going to wing it – *it is only one slide, anyway.*

As the presentation was winding down, we did a brief recap of our "Three Pillars of Widsom," followed by a final video of highlights of all the new programs for the upcoming season. The video was wonderfully edited and designed to be the capstone of the evening. It ended and the audience applauded wildly. Mission accomplished.

Then, the CEO strode out on stage and quieted the applause so he could deliver his final two slides explaining the details of the two new productions. His last section lasted perhaps two to three minutes, but it very successfully sucked all the energy out of the crowd that had been building for the last hour.

At the after party, there was much discussion among audience members about how "weird that was" and "not knowing when to quit," and "that guy really likes to hear himself talk." It was a shame that a really fine presentation would be remembered almost solely for its awkward ending.

CHAPTER TWELVE

An example of O.R.S.O.N. in action.

A few years ago, a television network that I was working for had a large, poorly organized, and archaic programming archive. It was housed in a building that was in a different state than the network sales department. The housing costs were coming (in large part) from my marketing budget. I needed to fix the problem fast. It involved a complete rethinking of the way things were done and required selling several different people on the idea. Here was one of the first applications of the ORSON system that I ever used.

Overview
- The lease is coming up on the archive building.
- The new lease will be double the current one.
- We have little time and a lot of issues to deal with.

Research
- We are wasting money on rent, manpower, utilities, travel, and shipping.
- We are losing money through lost time in transit.
- We are providing our clients with an obsolete product.

Solution:

- Digitize the entire archive.
- Get rid of all the physical tapes and replace them with servers.
- House the servers in the same space as the sales department.
- Create links to the new data base so employees can download clips rather than order copies.

Opportunity:

- We no longer pay rent – *savings*.
- We no longer need the manpower - *savings*.
- We eliminate interoffice shipping - *savings*.
- We improve time management - *savings*.
- We provide a better quality product, faster and easier for internal and external masters.
- One time start-up cost will be more than covered by savings in less than six months.

Next Steps:

- The Vice President will build a time frame.
- The Marketing Director will create inventory list.
- The Information Technology Director will price and order servers.
- All key contacts will regroup weekly to update.

Results: The pitch was well received. The project was launched and completed. The results were deemed so successful that plan was rolled out across network's other properties.

Another Example of O.R.S.O.N. in action

I am sorry to use so many media examples but they are where I spent most of my formative years in the industry. A few years ago, I was consulting for a television network as the Upfront season was fast approaching. They were unsure if they wanted to do another dog-and-pony show, because they had spent a fortune on them in the last two years, and neither had resulted in significant revenue gains for them. Here is how I employed ORSON in this instance.

Overview

- Over a million dollars was spent for the last two Upfronts, and got very little revenue traction in return.
- The events themselves were poorly planned and executed.
- If you are going to remain flat in revenue, why bother spending the money again?

Research

- The network tried to write and produce the event internally, but did not have the resources.
- People were assigned unfamiliar roles and tasks – in addition to their existing duties, not in lieu of them.
- None of the "producers" had any relationships in the event-planning world to leverage.
- There were no relationships with any of the vendors hired. Thus no negotiating leverage, and top dollar paid for *all* services rendered.
- The event was produced by programming department and not sales – despite the entire audience being sales contacts and clients, resulting in a complete disconnect in terms of content.

- If you do not do an Upfront event, it sends a message (even if only a tacit one) that you are also not participating in the Upfront selling season.

Solution

- Hire a dedicated outside producer.
- Have producer to work in tandem with sales force to get messaging right.
- Direct programming and production to follow producer's plan.
- Allow producer to leverage professional relationships in all aspects of the process: site rental, A/V, teleprompting, and catering.

Opportunity

- You no longer lose massive productivity from staff for four months – *savings*.
- Your message will be on target and client-centric.
- By leveraging the producers existing relationships:
  - Your rental will be vastly less expensive.
  - Your A/V costs will be vastly decreased.
  - Your catering costs will have decreased.
- You will have an event to be proud of, not embarrassed about.
- The producer fee will be more than covered by production and process savings.
- The overall budget will be half the previous year.
- Sales will see revenue increase as a result of a successful Upfront event.

Next Steps

- Engage the producer.
- The producer will build a time frame with the Director of Sales and the head of production.
- An Event Run-down will be agreed upon.
- Based on above, a budget will be developed.
- Division of labor will be agreed upon and duties will be assigned.
- All key contacts will regroup weekly to update.

Results: A producer was hired. The project was launched and completed. The event was a rousing success resulting in the network's most successful Upfront selling season in their history.

(Producer was offered full time position as SVP of Marketing)

CHAPTER THIRTEEN

Final Thoughts

As I stated in the opening, we live in an era when the ability to stand before an audience and deliver an impactful presentation is an increasingly valuable commodity. Despite the digital revolution, teleconferences, video conferences, Skype, webmeetings, webcasts, etc., nothing has replaced face to face communication as the single most powerful and persuasive communication tool we have.

Your body and your voice remain the primary medium of exchange of information. It is important to remember that language is critical but will always remain secondary to the entire package – it plays a supporting role.

Years ago, everyone's basic education contained public speaking – it was considered *de rigor*. Those days are long gone, and even at the college level, only very preliminary training is offered. The pendulum has swung drastically in the other direction – I cannot begin to list how many presenters have told me that they believe that they speak better, and more effectively, with less preparation. Counting on some divine inspirtation to provide a cogent flow of oration is not only a dangerous business, it is also reckless and irresponsible business.

Obviously, we may not all possess the capacity to become great orators, but with training, practice, and the desire to improve and purposeful application, we can become effective presenters. It is important to remember that it cannot, and will not happen, through gimmicks, tips, short-cuts, or merely reading books (even this one).

With honesty and authenticity as the goal, the key to being an expressive presenter is to remain supple, flexible and sensitive. I have endeavored to provide readers with a no-nonsense practical system that should deliver results immediately, but it is equally important to never lose sight of the fact that the idea is for readers to find their own path, their own style. It is important to adapt these principles and make them your own, rather than import them and force them to fit over or within their style. In the end, only that will give the presenter the complete freedom to create and invent within the structure of their presentation or speech.

CPSIA information can be obtained at www.ICGtesting.com
Printed in the USA
LVOW07s0049190315

431173LV00004B/239/P

MAR 2 7 2015

9 781628 651607